Rhythmic Thoughts and Recollections

Derek McKinstry

First published 2023 by Derek McKinstry

Produced by Independent Ink
independentink.com.au

Copyright © Derek McKinstry 2023

The moral right of the author to be identified as the author of this work has been asserted.

All rights reserved. Except as permitted under the *Australian Copyright Act 1968*, no part of this publication may be reproduced, stored in a retrieval system, or transmitted in any form or by any means, electronic, mechanical, photocopying, recording or otherwise, without prior written permission from the publisher. All enquiries should be made to the author.

Cover design by Derek McKinstry
Edited by Daina Lindeman
Internal design by Independent Ink
Typeset in 11/16 pt Adobe Garamond Pro by Post Pre-press Group, Brisbane

978-0-6459476-4-9 (paperback)
978-0-6459476-5-6 (epub)

For John, a brother, a father, a husband, a partner, an uncle, and a son.
A gentle soul who was loved by all. You are so sorely missed.

The first poem I wrote was for our brother John and is called Dark Place. It has taken me six years to write these poems and I have had support from many people over this time, and the following are a few who I wish to thank.

To Marina for your patience with me over the years it has taken to write this book

To Allison and Graeme for all your support

To Reena for your continued encouragement which inspired me from the outset

To my mates Bill and Phil for allowing me to discuss my writing over years of catching up for breakfast and lunch

To Kara for your openness and honesty that inspired more than a few of these poems

To Jen for the time you took to read my poems

To Con for prompting me to finally decide to self-publish

Contents

Nature

Balance Of Nature	3
Brand New Day	4
Burning Desire	5
Calm, Still Days	6
Calming Place	7
Feeling Life	8
Magic Place	9
Magic Sol	10
Moon Time	11
Mother Earth	12
Mountain Range	13
Natural Beauty	14
Nature's Stories	15
Plants	16
Salty Seas	17
Seasons	18
Soul To Sol	19
Speed Of Light	20
The Big Bang	21
Tree Of Life	22

Love

A Mother's Love	25
Chosen One	26
Desire	27
Embrace Me Now	28
Friends	29
I've Told You	30
Lift Of Love	31
Longing	32
Love	33
Love-struck Fool	34
Love Universal	35
Love's Passion	36
My Soul Is Sold	37
Secret Lovers	38
Strength Through Love	39
Sweet Love	40
Tempt	41
Thinking Of You	42
This Love	43
Waiting For The Day	44
When Love Is Strong	45
With Friends	46
Words Of Love	47

Grief

Abandoned	51
Acceptance	52
Calm Will Come	53
Dark Place	54
Dark To Light	55
Grief	56
Letter To A Friend	57
Loss	58
Lost Love	59
Love And Loss	60
Meaning	61
No God In Sight	62
Solace	63
Tell Me God	64
This Day	65
Time Of Sorrow	66
To Live To Give	67
Tombstone	68

Discrimination and Aggression

A Diary	71
Camp Slave	72
Conflict	73
Difference	74
Evildoers	75
Excluders	76
Golden Age	77
Hate-filled Flags	78
Mad World	79
Manipulator And Dictator	80
No Disunited States	81
No White Supremacy	82

One World	83
Paths To War	84
Peace Is Ours To Make	85
Race	86
Resilience	87
Retribution	88
Talk Of Slaves	89
Teachers	90
The Cult	91
The Fighters	92
The Jester	93
True Strength	94
Wars	95
Wars For Wealth And Power	96

Power, Wealth and Greed

A Time To Share	99
Automation	100
Communists And Fascists	101
Corrupted Power	102
Defiance	103
Full Control	104
Futures	105
Greed	106
Health And Wealth	107
Leaders	108
No Freedom Borrowed	109
Power	110
Structures	111
The Muddle	112
The Players	113
The Red Flag	114
Troubled Youth	115
Unbalanced	116
Values	117

The Human Condition

Abuse	121
Actors	122
Ancient Greeks	123
Betrayal	124
Champion's Heart	125
Colonisers	126
Come Together	127
Competition	128
Competitor	129
Country Girl	130
Dancing	131
Deception	132
Dog	133
Egomaniac	134
Failure	135
Families	136
Forty-Two	137
Full Circle	138
Gangs	139
God Of Guns	140
Gun Lobby	141
Happiness	142
Holidays	143
Homeless	144
Isolated	145
Jaded	146
Journeys	147
Justice	148
Meetings	149
Music	150
Natural Leader	151
Of Ants And Antelopes	152
Outrage	153
Party Girl	154
Pompeii	155
Random Nights	156
Retreats	157
Security	158
Ships of State	159
Slave Within The State	160
Spacecraft	161
Sporting Life	162
Suspicion	163
The Bully	164

The Drug Addiction	165
The Grind	166
The Tasks	167
The Walls	168
Toxic Leader	169
Vice	170
Wahine – 10 April 1968	171

Spiritual

Atheist	175
Blind Faith	176
Complexities of Belief	177
Creation	178
DNA	179
Doctrines	180
Evil Deeds	181
Faith In Love	182
God Of Love	183
Hallelujahs	184
Heaven And Hell	185
Holy Wars	186
Holy Water	187
In God's Name	188
Rome	189
Spirit Time	190
Spiritual Energy	191
State Of Mind	192
The Balance	193
The Godless	194
The Good Book	195
The Puzzle	196
Virtue	197

Introspection and Reflection

Age of Wisdom	201
Change	202
Chasing Dreams	203
Childhood Home	204
Childishness	205
Complimentary Insecurities	206
Confronting The Past	207
Conspiracy Theory	208
Doubt	209
Empty Roads	210
Facing Fears	211
Freedoms	212
Fungi	213
Happy Days	214
Helping Hands	215
Homestead	216
Kapiti Coast	217
Leaving	218
Loneliness	219
No Fear	220
Normal	221
Of Mystery And Magic	222
Other Worlds	223
Peace of Mind	224
Perceptions	225
Resistance	226
Rhythmic Thoughts And Recollections	227
Sacrifice	228
Self-Belief	229
Self-Worth	230
Sleepless Nights	231
Spaced Out	232
Spending Time	233
Spurned	234
Sun-filled Days	235
Sweet Dreams	236
Temper	237
The Amazing Kreskin	238
The Devil In The Shoelace Pie	239
The Verge	240
To Wander	241
Trauma	242
Trust	243
Wellington	244
Words Of Rhyme	245

Balance Of Nature

The birth of a child to this world brings a joy, a balance that equals the girls and the boys

All over the globe equal numbers displayed, but what is the source where such balance was made

To some they will state just as plain as can be, from a spiritual being we're unable to see

And all that belongs to earth, water, and air, forms part of this presence, of this they declare

The physical being like some spiritual daughter, random and wild but with balance and order

The good and the bad Mother Nature can bring, this force full of life being the soul of all things

This balance of nature that can bond like a mortar, but what we now see is destructive disorder

When the lushness of forest to a wasteland is turned, it's our hope for the future we continue to burn

The desire for our greed we embrace with a zest, the balance of nature being the thing that we test

Ignoring the risk seems the height of insanity, while the future we make is a climate calamity

And all that we hear is just squabble and noise, yet it's right on the edge we're so desperately poised

No longer in balance, nature brought to the brink, not an ark for the future but a raft that could sink

To be of this earth we are born for survival but of balance with nature we now need a revival

It's now we must show to this earth that we care, for there is no other world that we share

Brand New Day

The first rays of the sun at dawn, it's these that you now greet
The grass so green that fills the lawn, the dew upon your feet
The trees that seem so large and lush, a peacefulness this brings
Where what you hear is quietened hush and birds that softly sing
Of nothing else do you now care but of these natural features
The salty smell of seashore air, more sounds of nature's creatures
To sit upon the golden sand with sunlight's morning glory
This beauty drawn by nature's hand seems full of wonderous stories
The roar that comes from pounding waves that crash upon the shore
It's this you find your soul now craves, of nature you want more
You stroll upon the foreshore walk whilst joggers take their run
And couples have their casual talk as they enjoy the sun
These early morning sights and sounds that greet the brand-new day
With this it seems that you have found there is no better way

Burning Desire

Ripped and torn, turned to ashes and smoke, when they tear down a forest it's our anger they stoke
Untouched and unspoiled until stripped bare of all, a predatory passion by which they're enthralled
It seems there's no will and no way now to stop it, they wipe out a woodland for the sake of a profit
And the jungles and forests that produce our fresh air are left as just remnants that may disappear
Absorbed, engrossed, and indulged by their greed, destroying this beauty that will leave us bereaved
This slashing and burning without a reprieve, to these lungs of the earth that allow us to breathe
They tear down the forests then poison the air, while change to the climate is a thing they don't fear
Machines being made ready to bore down the hole, to invest in the future by burning more coal
Oil like treacle then refined gasoline, to which we're addicted, the world's nicotine
We plunder this earth as though without care, creating a wasteland where there's nothing to share
We need to extinguish this burning desire, discontinue our use of this carbon-based fire
Yet we fail to agree to impose joint decisions that will limit this use and these toxic emissions
The price of their profit is too much to pay, but still we have hope, and there's some who will pray
That soon we'll agree what's essential to say, we can't sell the future just to live for today

Calm, Still Days

The blissful sight of bright-filled days, with this the gloom is severed
The calm, still warmth and sun's sweet rays we wish to last forever
For sunlight brings a beauty here, to all the natural features
And with it all those thoughts of care for nature and its creatures
We've had our fill of cold and rain, no more of damp and dreary
As though such days could cause us pain, of these we are so weary
Sun's shining strength we wish to feel, the joy that this can bring
The melancholy that it heals, our spirits seem to sing
As though the sun now makes amends for when it did not shine
Time in the sun to share with friends, the days now long and fine
And with this time we seem so blessed, to bathe in all its glory
Without this in ourselves we're less, this sunlight makes our story
So bring to us these long, sweet days, for there we know we'll find
Those days which bring that warm, sweet haze will give us peace of mind

Calming Place

Spending time for things to gather, so many things that should not matter
When we all share the need to strive, for time that makes us feel alive
The warming sun, the gentle breeze, such feelings that will make you pleased
With birds that sing and pets at play, these things that make a perfect day
Relaxing time that you deserve in gardens, parklands, or reserves
That calming place where stress is lost, which brings a joy that has no cost
Where all the things you hear and see, can fill your senses and yet they're free
With others there being much the same, who share the reasons for why they came
How all the flowers and all the flora appear to have a sumptuous aura
Those perfect plants and tall, lush trees, seem there to set your mind at ease
Where to compare no judgement's passed as you relax on soft green grass
With nature seeming at its best, a place you feel at once at rest
At times you need a change of pace that takes you to this calming place
To feel the air so quiet and still, and there you stay to have your fill

Feeling Life

To spread their seeds or find a mate, to reproduce, to procreate
Conditioned now to grow or strive it's this we judge to be alive
With higher life being on the move through use of feet, or wings, or hooves
On legs to crawl, to run or stand, to swing through trees by using hands
What seems to us more close and real, is life that shows it knows or feels
A higher force when life has motion, a higher being through raw emotion
But now it seems we have no care for forms of life that blankly stare
As though they seem not quite so whole, these creatures deemed without a soul
When not being seen so self-aware we disregard their stress and fear
Long used for food or as a tool it's to these creatures we're often cruel
For hurt and pain they seem selected and what they feel is not respected
Could deep despair or pent-up rage be things they feel when penned or caged
What seems to some a vacant stare is still deserving of our care
Some wish a time where we could see from cruelty life that feels is free

Magic Place

So many wonderous things to see, how beautiful the sights
Of magic mountains by the sea, of days being warm and bright
That coarse and black volcanic sand, which traps the sunlight's heat
On this you feel you cannot stand, as though it burns your feet
Of rugged hills and fertile plains, of valleys full of mists
So teeming being the drenching rain that soaking land then slips
A dazzling range of snow-capped peaks, of forests and fiords
These awesome sights that you now seek, with nature there's accord
Of rivers wide that run so clean down to the Tasman Sea
As though this way it's always been and permanence we see
The forests that are so benign, no creatures that can harm
Their lushness that can seem so fine, that brings to you a calm
Of farms being fenced by country roads, to feel the slower pace
To shed the stress of heavy loads, in such a magic place

Magic Sol

A brilliant sight where all is bright, the glory of sun's shining light
As though a god, at times revered, our sun that warms and sometimes sears
Without you life cannot exist, through all our time your power persists
Your seething energy being radiated, the force of life invigorated
When shining are the light-filled days, life soaks up all your magic rays
Where all will need, and some will crave this light of life in which to bathe
Pure magic surely is your role, our great and mighty shining Sol
From dust they say that you were formed, a stardust where all life was born
But not to know how came to be, the dark void filled with energy
These suns that fill our universe seem from some holy sacred verse
Long in our history we have found a reverence to which we were bound
A shining god that seemed eternal, with searing heat though not infernal
Yet now we know with hearts and minds, your might and power shall then
    decline
One day a dream perhaps we'll chase, to find another home in space

Moon Time

Earth's shifting sands and mountain range, the moon through time so little changed
This moon we see there in the sky, the ancients saw with their own eyes
Such countless souls have gazed upon this silent moon that brightly shone
For permanence it has been selected and to our past it is connected
As days and weeks and months fly by, we see a change in clear night skies
Of crescent moon and then full face, such changes seem of a rapid pace
Of life we rush to have our fill, this moon it sits serenely still
Its presence felt in history's pages, a witness to the birth of ages
And all through time we've been intrigued, of mystery we were not fatigued
When moonbeams seem so softly bright, they lift us up towards their light
Of vision shared we then would talk, upon the moon we soon should walk
The moon has brought a time it seems, where we can realise all our dreams
The tide of time set by its pace, this sight with which emotion's laced
Its gift that makes some lovers swoon, when hearts seem set beside the moon

Mother Earth

A bright-lit sun to light your face by which you gleam in darkened space
An air of mystery and mystique which makes it seem that you're unique
As though all life is your creation, through tempests, trials, and tribulations
From you we see the power of living, a truth to life that's geared for giving
But some it seems will only take, your gifts to life they then forsake
What you create they will destroy by powerful means at their employ
Corruption that controls their minds now sways to crush what's good and kind
Sweet nature's gifts being precious honey consumed by all empowering money
To lies they'll give some crude construction to mask the truth of their destruction
With greed they'll try to hide through stealth the true cost that creates their wealth
They care not for our place of birth and fear not for our Mother Earth
This planet that we call our home it seems to most sits all alone
That there's no other place to live, to this there's little thought they give
No other place for which to run, for Mother Earth we must be one

Mountain Range

Your view of life seems rearranged when in your sight sits mountain range
Of snow-capped peak and lush filled valley, too many there for you to tally
The snow and ice of mountain's cold, that makes for feelings warm and bold
Majestically it now enthrals, its greatness that won't leave you small
And yet so calm, devoid of strife, as though a gift that's brought to life
How everything seems crisp and clear when in this clean, fresh mountain air
And when you find those mountain streams through forests that are flowing
You feel as though it must be dreams that nature now is showing
As what it is that you can see seems perfect in design
The beauty of these trees and streams that all seem so benign
As though transfixed by what you see, you take the time to stare
No thoughts of what to do or be, of this there's little care
For in this calm relaxing place you feel at once at rest
It's there you find that slower place, with nature at its best

Natural Beauty

With beauty you have always known of how it gleams with richness
To wish that nothing else be shown, for this your sight now itches
This beauty seen for you a must, with this your soul seems risen
A naturalness in which you trust, a clarity of vision
This beauty comes in many forms that glow with awe and wonder
The thrilling flash of lightning storms with rolling sounds of thunder
A lushness that can seem instilled through mists and sweeping rain
Of forests now with fauna filled, diversity to gain
The stillness of a cold clear lake reflecting what is seen
A desert where the sun will bake with plants as flecks of green
Of oceans breaking on the shores where sand dunes seem so golden
With all of this you want for more, of beauty being beholden
The sun sets in the evening sky and fades away the day
The moon that slowly rises high and takes stale thoughts away

Nature's Stories

Of all the glories now displayed, as though being stories nature made
A darkness that has turned to bright, of starkness now a soft warm light
As nature brings these depths of feeling it's then you know a strength of healing
Beholden now to nature's power, with feelings stolen by a flower
Of all of this will nature bring, you feel embraced as birds will sing
It fills the bowl and brims the cup, it takes your soul and lifts it up
For it's your soul that seems to fly, uplifted on a natural high
No more of sadness or to cry, contentment being the cause to sigh
Reflections shimmer from a lake to make the time you wish to take
This beauty that is bright and bold, it seems to have you in its hold
Of trees that stand so stout and tall, of fountains now being waterfalls
Majestic is this sun-filled scenery, so full of lushness and of greenery
When evening draws the close of day in vibrant colours pink and grey
You feel the glow of nature's glory, as though some never-ending story

Plants

What should we make of nature's plants and all the life they bring
Those vines that snake as though by chance seem such a natural thing
How is that these plants adapt to challenge causing change
In soil their anchored roots are wrapped, while seeds of life will range
Of insects that they will attract, a bargain for the deal
And those repelled if they attack, you'd swear these plants can feel
In varied climates they'll survive, like sentinels of old
With liquid water they will thrive, but ice being far too cold
Our lives depend on nature's plants, their goodness that we use
It's of our lives we play with chance if nature we abuse
Though plants can give us so much food and let us breathe fresh air
It seems that some are in the mood to give no thought to care
But care is what we now must make, for plants we need more feeling
As it's our future that's at stake and nature now needs healing

Salty Seas

All life on earth that came to be, of water, ground, and air
First life we know came from the sea, this truth we now declare
These seas at first of waters fresh that filled up the surrounds
But over time this freshness less with seas of salt being found
So many years of pounding seas to break upon the shores
And how through pounding rock will be, laid open to its pores
Through eons days of crashing waves, resources being unlocked
The source of what our bodies crave, the salt unlocked from rock
And on these salty seas we'd sail, exploring and then trading
A harvest's catch or harpooned whales, these seas of wealth for raiding
But now it seems we've reached a time when seas can seem depleted
Commercial contest makes us find the natural world depleted
These ancient seas that we abuse with little thought or caring
It's time that we decide to choose the naturalness of sharing

Seasons

It seems too long this winter's gloom and change you now wish seen
Closed up inside some heated room, how dreary life has been
With brightness just a light or lamp, of this you want no more
As all the cold and all the damp have sapped you to your core
When sunlight shines on soft white snow, a truly awesome sight
It's then you'll feel a winter's glow and days will dazzle bright
But now you wish for days of spring, for change being on its way
And all the joy that this will bring with warm, sweet, scented days
Of colours from the flowers that bloom and less of drab and grey
You wish that soon such days would loom, and on new lawn you'll lay
To hear the birdsong in the air when brown has turned to green
A landscape changed from stark to fair, for this you're now so keen
To want for warmth and longer days, no better seems a reason
Renewal of nature on the way with changes to the season

Soul To Sol

Our sun that holds us here in place, so brightly fixed in darkened space
The light we see like golden rays that brings to us the best of days
The radiant energy of its orb, which all of life can then absorb
This sun to warm but not to sear, protection through an atmosphere
No greater power than that of solar, of life it is the true controller
Of rhythms that can seem eternal, life in light and then nocturnal
As though a god to whom we'd pray, to turn each night again to day
That this has lost its special magic, to some can seem no less than tragic
No more to dance on sacred sun days, it's rest before some stolen Mondays
Much less a tribute to the soul, but still we seek what makes us whole
Emerging from the cold night's dark it's in the light we make our mark
With hopeful and inspiring stories that take in sunlight's golden glories
These shining rays will have their way, our spirits rise to greet the day
The place we find so bright and warm is where the bonds of love will form

Speed Of Light

This theory of the speed of light, which plays a trick upon our sight
The stars at night so bright and clear, although in view are now not there
The theory that they wish to teach us, is light will take so long to reach us
That now it seems our eyes have lied, for twinkling stars have long since died
They say that what we should believe is starlight that our eyes receive
Is nothing but some grand illusion, the ghost of long-past nuclear fusion
But if these stars have disappeared, then this should be a thing to fear
For if it's true, then what we face, is forever now being lost in space
To some this theory's science fiction, and in itself has contradiction
When caught inside some deep black hole, to speed of light this brings a toll
For light's then trapped by gravity's power, and there is no constant speed per hour
Entombed by gravity's powerful might, these black holes have no light to sight
To reach the stars should be our quest, light theory's what we then will test
These stars we see someday we'll reach, it's this belief that we should teach

The Big Bang

The theory of the great big bang, the time and place where all began
The beginning of the universe, as though some scientific verse
But still there is no theory stated of how this big bang was created
For all this power where was the source, that lit the dark with massive force
And how and when does this all end, we also cannot comprehend
For as there being an edge to space, how can we think of such a place
Perhaps there is no end at all, no degradation from which to fall
When galaxies have stopped their spinning, they come together for a new
    beginning
In fields of gravity they join in place, then form a critical mass in space
An explosive force, within its core, bursts out to fill the void once more
And life that's been and gone before with this renewal comes back once more
Through power and might this great revival, this blinding sight of life's survival
The force of life to bring its might, a beating heart this pulse of light
Where once was life again will be, but these are things we shall not see

Tree Of Life

The branches on the tree of life, of birds that nest and sing
Of beauty, struggle and of strife, all this will nature bring
Of deep cold lakes, or waters boiled, of forests vast and wild
Of fertile and productive soil, of storms then calm and mild
With flocks of birds and schools of fish, of wildlife and domestic
No greater wealth for which to wish, with nature so majestic
Volcanoes spewing molten rock, the force of nature's power
The seeds of life through soil unlocked, with rain a gentle shower
Of desert plains and mountain range, of lush and mist-filled valleys
But now we see such speed of change and hope that nature rallies
For though we feel we have great strength, to nature we belong
Our time on earth is short in length, it's nature that is strong
Destruction seems to be our course; through greed some seem so feral
In nature all life has its source, ignore this at your peril

A Mother's Love

A passing care shall not suffice this love requires some sacrifice
For in her thoughts her greatest care is how the ones she loves will fare
That fortune should not choose to smile upon the well-being of her child
This being a mother's greatest fear, that harm could come to those held dear
For when it comes to push and shove, is it not true a mother's love
Is such a bond that's tightly curled to bar the harshness of the world
It's then she shows such great concern with threats to face or from these turn
And of herself how much she gives, this love has changed the way she lives
But never will she ever hide the love that makes her swell with pride
Of those achievements great and small, such joy it is to share them all
And when it's time for letting go she tries to not let feelings show
For always they will still belong, a mother's love forever strong
No firmer bonds there'll ever be than love that's shared with family
For father, sister or for brother, this love is nurtured by your mother

Chosen One

It's from the time that we first met this different path it then was set
You changed the ways in which I live through all the love you gladly give
And what I see with all this change is how I lived now seems so strange
I know our love is deep and strong and it's with you that I belong
It's now I've found what I have sought, these ties of love they have me caught
No other place for me to run, with you I've found my chosen one
I know my love for you is real and with my heart this love is sealed
It's now I know what love can be, it's my desire that you've set free
These passions there that we'll explore, our love revered, admired, adored
Of this I'll tell you now my sweet, your loving charms I gladly greet
And with these words I'll now say more, my heart I lay down at your door
Within my life is where you fit, my soul's the throne on which you sit
It's now I've found what I have sought, these ties of love they have me caught
No other place for me to run, you truly are my chosen one.

Desire

Why should you try to be so coy when what can be is such sweet joy
To gaze but with it stale inaction, and all the while this strong attraction
The comfort sought of skin stripped bare, of bodies' warmth being closely shared
Sweet sensual touch so softly felt, from strong desires defences melt
Sole focus now being by your side with all the rest then put aside
A closeness sought with open arms, now bound by all these chains of charms
A longing that your thoughts will feed without concern where this may lead
This warm embrace and loving hug, it's at your heart these feelings tug
It seems as though you can't resist, of moves to make your mind insists
All thoughts of caution soon will fold when passion has you in its hold
A spark that flamed to be a fire, such beauty framed with strong desire
And how it seems this sweetest sight has cast the dark to bring the light
From senses now emotions flow and then you reap what they will sow
Embrace it all without a care, now is the time you feel you'll dare

Embrace Me Now

Embrace me now this quiet still night, enchanting love I cannot fight
As though unseen, without a sound, by ties of love I find I'm bound
This lustful love's placed high above, far more the hawk than of the dove
Such strong desires sweep down to claim, this yearning want being there
    to blame
Embrace me now dark spiritual night and place my love within my sight
The sweetest sight which with it brings, to feel as though my senses sing
From at their core emotions soar with passions that cry out for more
Then cast adrift, deprived of grace, these feelings too forlorn to face
Embrace me now this hallowed night before I fall from such great heights
To depths of darkness and despair when whom I love will have no care
My mind these thoughts seem set to steal if all my dreams cannot be real
And all the outcomes then so bleak when this unanswered love I seek
Embrace me now blind sacred night and let this dark now turn to light
To seal the wound and heal the sore and never be forevermore

Friends

Friends when weather's not so fair, when seas of trouble boil
Are those who truly show they care, for friendship they will toil
It's to your side with ease they slide to catch you when you fall
For care's a thing they will not hide when for their help you call
It's with a friend that you'll be shown, both comfort and forgiving
To know that you are not alone, and life is there for living
True friends to share your hopes and dreams and that of which you fear
To bare your soul at times it seems with friends you feel you'll dare
When friends are true it's then you know of things reciprocated
That care is what you'll also show, no need for this being stated
Emotions that you come to feel when old friends you will meet
A friendship that is strong and real with gladness you will greet
So cheers to friends who make things fine and all the joy they bring
The laughter as you share the wine, once more again to sing

I've Told You

I've told you of the way I feel and how for me you make it real
So down to earth and true to heart, your sweetness that can light the dark
I've told you how I now believe in all the things I can achieve
Support and care you gladly lend to show how much you are a friend
I've told you how I see your face as beauty that's as fine as lace
My senses heightened by your sight, it's you that makes me feel so light
I've told you of my strong desire and all the ways that you inspire
With open arms it's you I greet, these passions strong and yet so sweet
I've told you now the way it seems and how you fill me full of dreams
Of all your charms that I adore that make me feel this want for more
I've told you how my soul you steal and with your sight my heart you heal
The truth of this I have to say, how much it is I love your ways
I've told you of the way you shine and of my wish to make you mine
Your brightness stronger than the sun, I've told you all and now I'm done

Lift Of Love

With spirits low and feeling weak a lift of love you need to seek
You know that you were not to blame and that for you there is no shame
So view yourself with kinder eyes and with yourself now empathise
Then break the binds which hold you fast, that tie you to a painful past
And look to find the many ways to make the most of precious days
With open heart and emotions bare, to risk more hurt yet have no fear
For without fear comes peace of mind, much more than comfort you'll then find
A passion that will make you bold, someone to hug and tightly hold
To wish them close and by your side and with each other to confide
To have this want to feel the love, that fits as though some sensuous glove
These feelings, they have always been, but love's much more than just a dream
We all need lovers, but in the end, you truly are your own best friend
So for yourself you need to care, and feel the love you wish to share
It's then you'll find an open door to love that's blind to any flaw

Longing

In visions now your dreams are bathed with all the memories you have saved
And when the day seems dark as night you turn once more to your mind's sight
Of beauty dazzling sharp and bright that seems to dim all other light
Such perfect fullness in your sight, a power so soft with subdued might
All else as though it's in a haze, this beauty that will hold your gaze
Of all these charms you will attest, of beauty that outshines the rest
This vision fixed in your mind's eye, such longing that can make you sigh
Calm streams of thought, enticed by looks, can seem to turn to babbling brooks
You wish once more to have the chance to feel again your heart to dance
To rhythms where your soul will sing and all the joy that this will bring
To feel the touch so soft and warm, where all your senses there will swarm
To be so close and curled so tight and then to wish for endless night
When all these thoughts you cannot shake, then what it seems you'll need
    to make
Is for your dreams to now come true, this seems the only course for you

Love

This love they say shall conquer all, a precious gift that will enthral
Where some would gladly seek to sell their souls to feel its magic spell
With want is how they feel impassioned, through strong desire their feelings fashioned
A loose free will the thing employed when cravings fill an empty void
Much less a wish but more a lust, this need that makes some feel they must
As though they cannot rise above these depths that speak to them of love
But this is when true love is lost, for love can never have such cost
To prey upon you with a stealth and take from you a strength and health
For love is not of lust or vice, true love is full of sacrifice
To take more than you wish to give can never be the way to live
This special feeling for which we thirst begins when you put others first
When of ourselves we wish to share, we gladly show how much we care
With love we feel that we belong, through love when weak we're then made strong
It's love that lets us see the light and darkened days will then turn bright

Love-struck Fool

This restlessness again last night, your face once more in my mind's sight
My thoughts seem fixed in your direction with feelings filled with strong affection
But I implore, you should not dare, of what you know with others share
With only you I'll show my thoughts, of when or why or what is sought
To me you're sweet and yet so strong and it's your love for which I long
Embracing more than just your smile, to wait now seems it's worth the while
This loving care that fills your face, your beauty with its grace I chase
I see your soul behind your eyes and sweetness there it also lies
To see you I shall never tire, your beauty truly does inspire
For when I hold you in my sight the days can seem so warm and bright
When of my mind I've no control, emotions then can take their toll
These thoughts of you that now take hold to render me both weak and bold
This passion that you make me feel as though my soul I'd let you steal
A strong desire that will not cool, it's now I seem some love-struck fool

Love Universal

It's this that I have come to see through prime perception's prism
Of wonderous things that now can be, of beauty and clear vision
Of starlit glories filling space, of distant and of time
Which wait there for the human race, being pure and good and fine
The strength we find in love's sweet verse that brings us all together
Our future in this universe will only then get better
A time being seen of righteousness through love and understanding
Of this there can be nothing less, of this we are demanding
No wars or sores from want of more, of truth no more betrayal
That goodness shall be at the core, without this we shall fail
It's then we'll see what we can be, love's strength to bring the light
No toll from war or greed's cruel fee, no more to hate and fight
Division now we need to shun, the truth of this to face
Together we shall be as one, for we're the human race

Love's Passion

It's strength of love we wish to share with those we hold so close and dear
A love that brings its force to bear which steers a course that's bound by care
To take us to the place we heal and let us know our love is real
And there to find how we discover this love that binds us to each other
It's you I find to be the best, I have no mind for all the rest
It's now I'm caught by love's persistence and for release I feel resistance
This strength of feeling holds me here to share my love without a fear
For I can say I've truly seen such light-filled days as though a dream
So quickly does the present pass, we wish it still within our grasp
To be the host of what can be, our strength of love it's then we'll see
Of sorrow we will feel the least, tomorrow shall we dine or feast
A sweet-filled dish of love so blessed, it's now we wish for nothing less
It's when love seems so full and fine it's without haste we taste its wine
From pleasure's cup we sweetly sup and feel love's passion lift us up

My Soul Is Sold

These strength of feelings run so deep, such joyfulness I wish to keep
They tell me all I need to know and it's my love for you I'll show
You make me feel such love for you and what I feel is real and true
This love the thing that I adore, which makes me wish and want for more
Emotions high that seem to flow, no more to sigh from feeling low
With love we climb a gentle slope that brings with it the gift of hope
It's with this love that we belong, these feelings soft and yet so strong
Of hurt and pain our love to smother, our love a shield of gentle cover
It's with your love close by my side that lonely feelings now have died
It seems my heart through love has healed, an empty void is closed and sealed
Close comfort felt when by your side, on love's sweet path is where we ride
You bring a laughter to my fears so stay with me through all the years
And let me tell you now once more, your beauty truly I adore
Your soft caress that makes me bold has wealth by which my soul is sold

Secret Lovers

With a feeling of closeness that's truly adored it's the physical senses that must be explored

To act on emotions as though without care and this with a feeling as light as the air

A meeting of minds and of ultimate pleasure, craving the time they can share at their leisure

Sweet secret hours are the things that are stolen, with each to the other being bound and beholden

A love that creates such a beautiful mingling, a heartfelt embrace that can leave bodies tingling

With all other thoughts being left far behind when this is the way in which two are entwined

Their tender embrace, so soft, warm and smooth, to fall into place and to slide into groove

Their mutual desire and their yearning released, as though it is passion on which they will feast

This strength of desire they have need to express, with waves of emotion it reaches its crest

No thoughts to deny what their bodies confess as they yield to these senses of love at its best

This sensuous feeling to which they're addicted, as though it is passion by which they're afflicted

Struck down with these feelings, tormented, aggrieved, but never to wish for a pause or reprieve

To many great lengths these lovers will chase the spiritual feeling of this sensual embrace

And for all of the while, and for not one day less, the sanctuary they seek is this sweet soft caress

Strength Through Love

It's when we hold each other dear to each we'll show our love and fear
An open and true trusting heart is how the best of journeys start
As though a rock, a strength, a shield, through this we find our love is sealed
If passing storms the future holds, this love shall bring its warmth to cold
But some will never share their fear, of this they feel they would not dare
To them a strength is full of macho, they act in haste with false bravado
Yet fear is held in their possession and sometimes met with blind aggression
To push and shove or rant and rave, it's this they feel will make them brave
This fear that's held is deep inside and from it they now want to hide
When words or thoughts they wish to silence, their only path seems one
    of violence
So who is now more truly weak, to some it seems it's not the meek
True strength being found in compromise, of this there can be no surprise
Of selfish thoughts to rise above, from truths of strength can then come love
Through sweet love's strength we show we care and more of this we'll wish
    to share

Sweet Love

Through strength of love we hold the key to all that we are seeing
To be the best that we can be, the essence of our being
And it's this love that keeps us strong when age surpasses youth
To bring us back where we belong, again to feel its truth
For love shall always plant a seed that grows and blooms with care
Which makes you know just what you need is love that you can share
And when it's this you wish to show, these seeds of love for sowing
Your heart it then begins to glow, you feel emotions flowing
At times in gentle soothing streams, or rivers that are swelling
As though to float upon your dreams when love is where you're dwelling
When sweet love's storm controls your mind, with willpower seeming sapped
It's at these times you then can find, this love it has you trapped
But love can never hold us down, though sometimes we may sigh
True love is like a precious crown that always lifts us high

Tempt

Desire with lust and vanity, these things seem set to trouble me
As though I have a strong intent to stay engaged with all that tempts
My conscience seems to be sedated, impassioned thoughts are then created
It's wilful lust with which I see, and with this lust such vanity
As though whoever I desire should also feel this burning fire
This passion that I long to share, of little else I seem to care
A movement and a grace within, a sensuous softness to the skin
Much more than sweetness to adore, a subtle strength to reach the core
Fine feelings first so soft and warm bring brazen thoughts where passion swarms
These senses now so strong and deep are feelings that I wish to keep
Such beauty there that strikes my sight with soft-felt blows I cannot fight
With actions primed and full of zeal, a lust controls the way I feel
Temptation makes it hard to cope, as though for me there's little hope
My mind seems full of thoughts that tempt, to chase me down until I'm spent

Thinking Of You

With you and I it's plain to see, we're living large in life's lush tree
And how we wish to feel the love, bestowed on us from high above
That what to us makes perfect sense is what you feel without pretence
Emotions raw, and though uncaged, not strutting on some actor's stage
With you it's now I feel I'm seeing the strength of naturalness of being
At times so calm and then abrupt, with truth that none can then corrupt
And how with you no one can steal your ways and means that make it real
This power you have at times so strong that guides you to where you belong
Your nature nurturing a child, to see the fun and feel it wild
And yet it's deep that you can care, a life that's lived being bound to share
Of fairness you will boldly state, which puts in place all thoughts of hate
Those times you wish to run and hide, such strength within you find resides
In downcast thoughts no time to spend when bright filled light is where we mend
Again to know of those who'll lend the trusted shoulder of a friend

This Love

This love that seeped into my soul to fill me up and make me whole
A thing that I cannot ignore, it's strength of beauty to the fore
This love now enters all my dreams and glows with shining soft sweet beams
To take me to that special place where love is what I wish to face
This love that comes as though with stealth to bring to me its treasured wealth
Of riches that I did not ask, a love I cannot hide or mask
This love that takes my will by force, emotions flow with love their source
Being swept up in love's path now seems a torrent full of gentle streams
This love that turns the cold to warm when strong emotions surge and swarm
And how I wish for evermore, this love to make my feelings raw
This love to me a precious gift which makes my sense of spirit lift
It's love that now I need to share, without it I shall feel despair
This love that makes me want to say how much it brightens up my day
Those mundane times they now have passed, instead sweet love is here at last

Waiting For The Day

It seems so long since I have seen your beauty full of spirit
And now my words, so ever keen, are poems full of lyric
Of how to me you seem so sweet, such softness in your face
It's now again I long to greet your beauty full of grace
A glow that seems so strong and clear with tenderness to find
The fullness of your flowing hair, your voice so sweet and kind
Much more than this is what I seek, to hear again your laughter
As though it's this I wish to keep, to linger long thereafter
The essence of your naturalness from gentleness is made
It's all these things I sorely miss, your beauty being displayed
And then to share the deepest thoughts, of all those long-held dreams
To try to make some sense of sorts of what this truly means
Your face at last again being seen, of this I want to say
Too long it seems that it has been, while waiting for the day

When Love Is Strong

When love is strong it seems so deep, forever long this love to keep
As though emotions chime and tingle, of hearts embraced, entwined,
    and mingled
Being caught in love you can't resist, no thoughts or words can then assist
Love's gentle hug and sensuous kiss, that make you feel you're bathed in bliss
The sweetest times for you to fashion, and then to shine in perfect passion
Consuming's how this love can seem, as though your life's become a dream
Love spins you in its serene dance, where conscious thought's more like
    some trance
To take you to that special place, to share an intimate embrace
As though love's essence you are breathing and there can be no thoughts
    of leaving
It's in each other's arms you lay and here is where you wish to stay
For such sweet time can have no toll as love then takes its full control
These feelings, strong and warm and bright, you know for you this love is right
What once seemed empty now is whole, to love you feel you'll give your soul

With Friends

How good it is to have a friend, a comfort borrowed or some to lend
With friends there is no need to act, and words may be of little tact
For friendship has a knowing trust and loyalty given is a must
In troubled times it's friends who stay, this given trust they won't betray
While others may become your past true friendship is a thing that lasts
A contract no one needs to sign but one that's real and warm and kind
With friends there is no need to hide, they know within what thoughts reside
You share your fear or show your pride, it's friends that you will let inside
They'll gladly give and take the time to make some days seem long and fine
Through friends you feel that you belong, a feeling that will keep you strong
It's friends with whom you'll share the date and take the time to celebrate
As though you'd wish forever after to feel the joy and share the laughter
When of ourselves we truly share it's then we show how much we care
It's friends that bring the light to you, without your friends what would you do

Words Of Love

From love there's some who turn away, they say their hearts are broken
Their thoughts and feelings shan't be swayed, no words of love are spoken
To risk more hurt they will not dare, their brows now tense and furrowed
They feel for them that none shall care, and deep within they've burrowed
When you can feel no love to give the emptiness is tragic
For you will find the life you live is now without some magic
To feel some love is what we need, this need being fundamental
For love alone can plant the seed to all that's kind and gentle
It's love we feel, which forms the key, to those for whom we care
An unlocked heart is what we see when love is what we share
With love we heal from all that's bad, of things we wish to banish
And of those thoughts that make us sad, with love they seem to vanish
This love that brings its shining sight to troubled times we face
The darkness that will turn to light when love's what we embrace

Abandoned

Your heart you pledged to love and trust but care now quickly fades
When all you had has turned to dust by love that's been betrayed
A coldness with a frosty chill is now communicated
And spoken words hang sharp and still, with harshness they are stated
Like shards of glass it's then they pass to tear your heart in two
This change has seemed to come so fast with walls being made for you
The shock so swift it takes your breath, this coldness leaves you gasping
The love you had has met its death, for comfort you are grasping
A silence as you speak no more, this message loud as thunder
It's now you know such hurt and sore with feelings torn asunder
Within your mind you're so confused, and anxious thoughts are swarming
You feel as though you've been abused, abandoned without warning
There is no cure that you may take, no gentle path to healing
Some say the best is what to make, the worst is what you're feeling

Acceptance

Acceptance is the word they use but you have come to see
This word is one you would not choose, with this you disagree
For to your core you have been rocked with all that you have lost
And it's your soul that has been shocked as now you count the cost
When all those days that seemed so fine no longer now can be
Sweet memories are for which you pine, such days again to see
It seems that life has lost its lustre, with lessening of affection
Now all your strength you'll need to muster, it's you that needs protection
To some it's faith that gives them strength when sad loss they must greet
While lonely days seem long in length they're sure again they'll meet
If faith has not yet come to you then wrap yourself with love
As love is there to comfort you, within and from above
To feel resigned, the words you'll find, that say how things now seem
To reach this point within your mind, a time of calm is seen

Calm Will Come

It's to these depths your spirit's shaken when from your life a loved one's taken
With all your strength and self-belief as though consumed by endless grief
And in these depths you're seeming mired, such sadness leaves you drained and tired
Your life can seem so darkly changed with feelings raw and rearranged
For what you feel is cold and stark and filled with all that's bleak and dark
As though you feel your heart will break and all your strength this loss will take
But calm will come when your mind sights a time that slowly brings the light
Being bright and warm and full of love, to wrap your soul as though a glove
Embraced by love emotions swarm, and through this love new hope will dawn
From dark-filled depths you'll rise above when you accept this gift of love
Sad days that seem forever longer, it's these that you will come to conquer
You'll share your pain with those who care and feel the love that stems the tear
For while through love it's grief we feel, this love's the thing that grief can't steal
It's in the light that you belong, where love will heal and keep you strong

Dark Place

The jagged edge, scars ripped through
Hearts laid bare because of you
Desperation took your life
Unleashed a storm of grief and strife
Long dark nights that stole your light
Left a shell when the day was bright
This darkness that you tried to bare
Made you anxious and gave you fear
All the beauty that cannot be
When the dark is all you see
Is beauty that will not be missed
When staring down the dark abyss
For the hurt you gave to those who loved you
For guilt you cause when thinking of you
For the grief and sorrow of our mother
I forgive and love you brother

Dark To Light

Alone you sit amongst the crowd, so silent when the rest are loud
Your feelings covered with a shroud, not shy but somehow not so proud
Importance seems that of a pawn, you feel you see how lines are drawn
A truth to you is seen to dawn and with it you become withdrawn
You try to not let feelings show, for now you're feeling lost and low
These feelings you would wish to stow, the ones where you can feel the blow
The light has dimmed in mists of rain, you cleanse but still the stain remains
You try so hard to make that gain, but fall again in fits of pain
Just where it is your mind has ranged has left you feeling raw and strange
But with this there is hope for change as feelings will be rearranged
For when it is you find the light it feels it has such power and might
No longer blind to strong clear sight, no longer fear to give you fright
No matter what the darkness tried, you know that doubts and fears have lied
Through all of this you have survived and to the light you've now arrived

Grief

This darkness now forever deep yet in itself will bring no sleep
Into its depths your soul will seep and with its weight it makes you weep
An anger that can make you seethe, this turmoil tests what you believe
You find no peace that will relieve this sadness as you start to grieve
The pain that's known will make you cry; with floods of tears you groan and sigh
To deep despair you feel you dive, and to this place you then arrive
A place that seems so dark and dense and all around is barred and fenced
This place there can be no pretence and where to you there makes no sense
Where all is wrong and nothing's right, the days are long but without light
You feel that you shall never sight some glimmer slowly turning bright
As though for you your fate is sealed, that in your heart you can't be healed
But while this now seems true and real in time this is not how you'll feel
Though you now feel your heart may break it's care that you should not forsake
It's strength through love we need to make, such strength this grief shall never take

Letter To A Friend

Hello dear friend and how are you, I know you've had so much to do
That all your time is filled with tasks, so questions are not raised or asked
It's to these duties you're resigned, they help so much to fill the time
And take the focus from the cost of what you had that now is lost
But now we near the festive season, to toil there's little need or reason
This time of feasting now the first without the joy for which we thirst
It seems that grief will not diminish, this sadness never seems to finish
With all this grief now so confronting, it's troubled thoughts that then
    come hunting
For with this loss you feel alone with little comfort now being shown
But it's with time you'll find some peace, the rawness of this pain shall cease
And though it's sadness you now greet, there's some who say again we'll meet
Dark thoughts should never hold the day, best keep them down and well at bay
So greet the sights and hear the sounds of places where some joy is found
Where friends will show they're thinking of you, and just how much it is they
    love you

Loss

Your tears now with this sadness shown seem like the waves which turn to foam
To break upon some lonely shore, a sea of tears yet still there's more
You feel too weak to bear the toll and cannot fill this gaping hole
Within your mind despair now lays, clear thought seems lost in fog and haze
Of nothing now you seem to care when who you love's no longer here
You grieve and mourn a loving soul and with their loss you don't feel whole
The one with whom you loved to share; this love now lost has stripped you bare
Long nights that leave you in a daze, direction now being like a maze
It's time that heals these wounds of love and from this pain you'll rise above
While in your eyes more tears are brimming, from loss we find a new beginning
The dark-filled time of endless night replaced by days that bring the light
To feel the warmth and sweet fresh air, now lessened is your deep despair
It's love that others gladly share, their love which shows how much they care
And when you feel this love that's shown, it's then you'll know you're not alone

Lost Love

The loss you feel that hurts and steals, emotions seeming shattered
What you had seen as true and real, your hopes and dreams now scattered
When lives are lived with love for others, without them we seem lost
An emptiness that grows and smothers, with loneliness the cost
This heartful loss that you must face, a sadness brought to living
Alone within an empty space, there's little thought to giving
But giving's what you need to share, it's this that makes us strong
To show how much you truly care, to know where love belongs
So free yourself from this despair and all that it will bring
From emptiness to bright fresh air, with songs that birds will sing
To soak up all the warming rays, good company to find
And how it is that bright-lit days can bring you peace of mind
We all will know of love that's lost, of ties by which we're bound
But time will show the truest cost is new love to be found

Love And Loss

There comes a time when you will find of love and loss they are entwined
A time when you will then discover they cannot be without each other
It's only then you'll have belief that without love you can't have grief
Of hurt that makes you feel you'll fall, when loss and grief will come to call
Of love's sweet picture full of gain now brushed with bruising strokes of pain
But all the darkness now seen painted shall never make your love feel tainted
For life we find will then insist that without love we can't exist
It's for this love we want for more, enough there never seems in store
And while at times we all must grieve, through love is how we all achieve
The beauty shown in how you live dependent on the love you give
Love's bittersweet when etched with pain but in your heart true love remains
It's loss that leaves us feeling hollow, this path that none would wish to follow
But this is not the journey's end and broken hearts in time will mend
Down to your soul you'll soon feel sure, love's purpose now being to endure

Meaning

This time that seems to make no sense, which leaves you feeling sad and tense
When love has pain it's then you find just how it is these two entwine
The one that feels such joyful bliss, this sadness for the one you miss
You cannot think of what you'll do or what this now will mean to you
For meaning simply can't be found, of this there is no sight or sound
A thing to which you'd gladly run, but on its own it needs to come
Though cherished is what you once had, your life means more than feeling sad
While hurt seems all there'll ever be, with time it's then you'll come to see
That from this hurt you will not fall as love and pain unites us all
And of this pain that we will feel it's from its hurt we all can heal
We lessen how it hurts and harms by reaching for each other's arms
It's meaning then that can be found, so simple and far from profound
You'll find this turns away the harm and with it brings a quiet, still calm
To build you up and make you whole, and give back purpose to your soul

No God In Sight

You think of all that you have lost, this turmoil leaves you turned and tossed
Disjointed thoughts now seeming crossed, you wonder how you'll bear this cost
It's raw emotion grief has sown, with pain that makes you sigh and groan
So hard to face this loss you're shown, its bleakness makes you feel alone
It's now you know life takes its toll no matter how you play the role
It tears you up and leaves a hole, to place a scar upon your soul
If life is just but what we see, what does this mean for you and me
For none as yet have found the key to life that's lived without a fee
When bright-filled light will dim and fade you ask yourself how God was made
Just how the ancient paths were laid, why all must leave when God has stayed
They say with faith you stay the course; some preach of this until they're hoarse
Of God being all of life's great force, where all that lives shall have its source
But where now is this god of light, this god of awe yet one of fright
This god of truth and righteous might, it seems there is no god in sight

Solace

It's this that leaves you shattered, with pain being all you know
Much more than bruised and battered, strong feelings leave you low
When all around are mountains bringing valleys to your soul
Your tears have flowed like fountains as though sadness is your role
Of all this pain you've spoken, of all this hurt you've seen
Your spirit has been broken and you yearn for what has been
But torrents that were flowing have turned to gentle streams
The light that dimmed is glowing as you drift towards its beam
A place of calm reflection, to this you'll then arrive
Which brings with it perception of the gift to feel alive
No more those depths of darkness, your mind now set to rest
You rise above the starkness and your pain is seeming less
Take solace now with loved ones and keep your spirits strong
The dark is what you need to shun, the light's where you belong

Tell Me God

Tell me God what to believe when now my soul is broken
And why it is when I must grieve no words from you are spoken
Why all the world seems full of pain and never a solution
With nothing ever to be gained from violent revolution
When all seems tainted and corrupt, contempt being shown to need
How sores that fester soon erupt when endless is their greed
So tell me God just what is faith when little seems of virtue
When chains of pain will choke and chafe and all seems to hurt you
They say for us you have a love and gentle is your being
When horror in our face they shove no gentleness we're seeing
So tell me God and I will listen to tales of shining light
How through you all must surely glisten with pure and righteous might
But now I'm seeming sad and lost and reeling from my feelings
As when I find I count the cost, so hard some sense of healing

This Day

This day again where I must think how close it brought me to the brink
And with such grief that I survived I'm yet to really feel alive
I steel myself against the feeling of how I wish some sense of healing
For what has passed seems little time, to truly say I'm feeling fine
I think back to what we once had and how this leaves me feeling sad
The days we spent, the time we shared, for you I know how much I cared
At times I cannot seem to find a calm that comes with peace of mind
For of this day I know its mark, it calls on feelings cold and stark
I miss the light so bright and strong and wonder now where I belong
It seems the day it has me caught, in feelings that control my thought
But of my light these thoughts shan't steal for in my heart it's time to heal
Where feelings shall not seem to stalk, with gentler paths for me to walk
So while again I'll know this day, my thoughts shall not be in harm's way
Whatever comes with sad reflection the strength of love will give protection

Time Of Sorrow

To feel alone with all your sorrow, why should you care for your tomorrow
For sorrow seems it will destroy those feelings that can bring you joy
Into such depths you seem to sink when joy is now to sadness linked
At times what seemed as light air has left you feeling deep despair
The future that your mind can sight seems starkly bleak and far from bright
And while this now seems real and true, this future's not the one for you
But all your strength is what you'll need for this sad time seems long indeed
Yet you will know of those who care and how your feelings you can share
With this will come the time you'll find a strength within that's calm and kind
That to this dark beyond control will bring a light that soothes your soul
This time of sorrow you now face, this loss that makes you feel displaced
In this raw form it will not last, the bleakness of this time will pass
For its with love that we are strong and through this love we all belong
It's on the shoulder of a friend the sadness of this time will mend

To Live To Give

When those you loved so much are gone, from this world passed away
At times so strong you feel you long that here we all should stay
Acceptance you had seemed to find, a peace of sorts being made
But now it seems within your mind, reactions were delayed
You wonder just what life's about, to this your thoughts are leaning
Frustration that can make you shout, when you can find no meaning
For meaning's at the core of life, for this we all will strive
With meaning we can deal with strife; it makes us feel alive
It need not be of high esteem, some special way of living
When love's the thing that you have seen, to love you then are giving
At times we all will feel a grief, some sadness to the day
But if in love you have belief such feelings won't hold sway
With love to give and care to lend, on this we all depend
So cherish now the time you spend with family and with friends

Tombstone

Your brother's death has made you think, into those depths you must not sink
No way to cross that great divide, to take your life by suicide
With strength of mind before the fall your castle now an empty hall
That precious feeling to belong the only thing to keep you strong
To be beloved by those that care, to shoo away and stem the tear
It's cherished love that brings the light, forgone despair as dark as night
Your brother's death has made you think, into those depths you must not sink
But from this dark you now must turn, more of this love the thing to yearn
When in your life there's love for giving, it brings such worth to life for living
With giving love it's then you'll find through love you have a strength of mind
To love your life and love to laugh a sweet and simple epitaph
When comes the time to leave alone let these words speak from silent stone
Embrace the gift of long sweet days, enjoy them all without delay
To trust and then to roll the dice, the journey to your paradise

Discrimination and Aggression

A Diary

A sweet child's written story of how she had to hide
And yet it's etched in glory when her tale is to survive
A pride that has a virtue, a tale that's told of love
When those in power will hurt you with harsh orders from above
But love could never save her, cruel fate she had to face
No one to be her saviour and she died because of race
When power's some evil doctrine, brutality is what they'll show
They'll have no fear of mortal sin, lay waste to all we know
In evil they will revel, as God's not on their side
More so it seems the devil in their darkened souls resides
Why should this ever be their wish, the murder of a child
To feast upon the poisoned dish, it makes them mad and wild
The lesson we must learn from this is how we share our fate
When what we share is then dismissed we harm ourselves through hate

Camp Slave

At first it seems you've been displaced through catastrophic error
But cruelty makes you seem disgraced with beatings full of terror
And of your life that once had been, of this there is no trace
An endless toil with hunger seen, it's this that you now face
Stripped bare of all, how far you fall, to depths of deep despair
No longer one who may stand tall, for you there is no care
A sadness where you feel forlorn, it's this you've come to know
Your clothes are torn, your shoes are worn, your feet freeze in the snow
Harsh work with quotas to be filled, of number, weight, and measure
To fail in this you could be killed, your torment forms their treasure
And then at night you'll wish to dream of restful days and slumber
Yet rest for you will not be seen when you're now just a number
But hope's the road your heart will drive, this hope that you'll be free
To feel this horror you'll survive and better days you'll see

Conflict

In conflict there's no normal life of which we can partake
No place to find devoid of strife or restful times to make
When all around is being destroyed, through this they wield their power
Where nothing now can fill the void, from brutal death to cower
When all that's good is turned to dust, in evil they will revel
Their spiteful deeds devoid of trust, which seem they're of the devil
For they will bring such dreadful might, through terror they are strong
Their name being held in fear and fright, to them we must belong
Of conquest they are never tired, nor war to have their fill
In blood-filled dreams it seems they're mired as ever more they kill
It's them they say that have been wronged, what's yours they need to take
It's full control for which they long, your freedoms are at stake
This conflict seems it will not cease, it's been this way through history
To join the fight to bring the peace is never contradictory

Difference

Those ancient paths along a line that seems to stretch forever
Genetic strands have us entwined, as though being strung together
This DNA that holds its sway for features of our races
We're not the same, so some will say, it's difference their speech chases
A difference should be celebrated, a spice being brought to life
But when for difference you show hatred, your cause is one of strife
A world of trouble this will bring to fellow human beings
Their hatred is a spiteful thing, when shameful acts we're seeing
And all that you will ever gain when actions are so baited
Is see the hurt and feel the pain from factions full of hatred
Some say they are the master race, in all that they achieve
Yet they are full of vile disgrace, when this they will believe
So stand against the hate-filled calls, their slogans full of spite
Together is how we stand tall, and hatred we shall fight

Evildoers

When might is full of righteousness against all evildoers
The irony they seem to miss, how easily evil lures
An evil they wished to defeat, the righteous path they chose
Reflection that their eyes must greet, they're now what they oppose
Yet all the while they'll try to find those words that justify
How they can force a change of mind, no matter who may die
With torture how they'll inflict pain, of truth to now confess
So hard the fight, but all that's gained is just some frightful mess
As countless victims sigh and groan, of lives once full now stolen
Of bullets, bombs, and buzzing drones, as though to fear beholden
They clearly never reach the end that justifies the means
More broken lives that cannot mend is what the outcome seems
And nothing is what they have learned from more of their mistakes
As though that all is to be burned, our future being at stake

Excluders

A world in pain and full of fires, with truths there are some strong deniers
That nothing's real and all is fake, their own small world they choose to make
The only truth is what they see and nothing else can ever be
With factual truths to be despised, for this is where their comfort lies
Minds being closed and blocked with fear, of other thoughts they would
    not dare
For strength to them is what they know, no other way you now can show
This weakness where they think they're strong, with feelings that they
    must belong
To be the same is what they share, an open view's too much to bear
They keep themselves within closed groups, some venture out as though as troops
To hurt and maim and set to right, those strangers who they choose to fight
They wish to force their cruel control, at times they seem devoid of soul
Such fighting has no truthful purpose, and long it seems will conflict curse us
For the weak and hurtful feeble-minded, have little thought with whom
    they're sided
It's with their violent hate-filled moods, they set their sights on to exclude

Golden Age

What we have seen by nation's will is how it's others some wish to kill
Of dispute they shall take no more and set the course being bound for war
As though it's this that makes things right, to take control through power and might
It's been this way through history's page but now we need a brand-new age
An age of strength through care and healing, and not by plunder's ruthless stealing
To be as one and shed our fear, and know this world is ours to share
How easily then we'd recognise a weakness that we should despise
The one where trouble's bound to start, by saying from you I am apart
We must be one and all united, if not we'll see destruction sighted
For when it is we stand alone to failure we are surely prone
To understand that beauty seen can be much more than what has been
Then stand upon the strife-torn stage and usher in our golden age
An age where we will find protected all that needs to be respected
Respect being based on love and care, of this who would not wish to share

Hate-filled Flags

Their hate-filled flags they proudly wave, through slogans they will rant
    and rave
They tell you how you should behave, it's you they wish to make a slave
They want the power to take control, to bend your mind and steal your soul
Of those they hate they'll stalk and troll and tell you that they're less than whole
They say it's others you must fear, for in their hearts they have no care
It's from your grasp they'll rip and tear those precious things that you hold dear
For with their lies they make you blind, plant poisoned seeds within your mind
To bring you to that place you find that others are not of your kind
Where those like you will make you strong, and it's to them that you must throng
For they can right what seems so wrong, no other place do you belong
But freedom is the thing that's died when you feel weak and take their side
There is no strength when we divide, and soon you'll find how much they've lied
It's care for others that holds the key to make the world we wish would be
So take the path where you will see it's love that truly makes us free

Mad World

A wilful destruction seems set in its place, threats that are real and which all may soon face

Armed conflict creating great chaos and strife with a terror that looms causing fear to be rife

Strongly is stated their wish for no harm, yet whoever shall fight they will promptly then arm

Weapons provided by those with the power and from this dilemma our leaders will cower

Warfare now being such a lucrative industry, no matter its purpose is death and much misery

Sights so obscene to wish eyes from our sockets shall never compare to the wealth for their pockets

When dismissive of care it is then that we fall, with misdeeds and murder at each other we maul

To crush then to plunder, to pillage and ravage, discarding the civil and embracing the savage

Without trust for each other we create insecurity, then no one is safe and of that there is surety

When acting with violence fear's flag is unfurled, desperate times are then brought to the world

All we shall reap from the seeds sown by wars are wounds that won't heal with slow-festering sores

Swirling and spinning in this destructive force with no paths seeming clear to create a safe course

Wonders we sight that can brighten the globe, but the light is disjointed as though cast through a strobe

We all to each other owe a duty of care and what we should show is being willing to share

Manipulator And Dictator

Their skills they will use to manipulate, to gather support to control then dictate
Their purpose being only to dominate, to spread a false message, the one full of hate
To fracture and part is how they'll begin, through different beliefs or the shading of skin
Perversely to point out diverse racial features, this makes us apart, so their false doctrine teaches
To whom is the god or how we will pray, made unholy beliefs and not some other way
The way that we look or the language we speak, so small is the difference that they spitefully seek
It's due to their difference, with lies they will claim, why others are always the ones we should blame
To be all the same they will say makes you strong, while fuelling your fears that you do not belong
But choosing to join will be made with great error, for soon you will find you're caught up in a terror
When fears will fully be reaching their peak, and voices are silenced with reluctance to speak
Then what will be seen in the world that they've made, is a distrust of others that will make us afraid
Through division they wish to control all the world, as insults and threats to the others are hurled
But be wise and aware of those words you may hear, and what they will say are the things you should fear
For having belief that we're not all the same is a life that is lived in contempt without shame

No Disunited States

Great inequality is what we now see, which does not belong in the land of the free
But poverty has links as though chains to a collar when stronger than love is the almighty dollar
This need for the dollar that has all the power, to make you or break you when paid by the hour
The want of the dollar so powerful and fierce, that what's now abundant can soon become scarce
It binds up the poor with a stark separation, creating division and a deep desperation
No more to be one but now disunited, and the words of your founders can seem to be slighted
How can it now be that your States once united seem so far apart and so deeply divided
A war between States that did not seem to end, these are the thoughts that division will lend
New flags being raised to bring cause to their gripes, to take from the power of the Stars and the Stripes
And as for the flag of those violent race-haters, when raising this flag it is they who seem traitors
And could it be race or is it just due to wealth, when slow to attend to your sick nation's health
As crisis appeared your responses were small, with failures in health it's your systems that fall
While now it can seem that you have no direction, we still look to you with such strength of affection
And we truly have hope that you'll soon come to see, united is what makes your great country free

No White Supremacy

Too easily seems how some will bring a fear that we can face
With slogans they will chant and sing how they're the master race
The swastika, that hate-filled flag, no longer in plain sight
With other flags is how they brag, you're special if you're white
The flags that we now see unfurled, pure chaos they'll create
All other races in the world are less than them they state
Some leaders have been keen to chase a nationalistic fervour
That this can seem being based on race caused little more than murmur
It's shock they feign, and great surprise, to find that they've unleashed
Behaviours that should be despised, a riotous angry beast
What is it that they think they'll gain from hate-filled separation
Embroiled in grief and hurt and pain, how can this be a nation
For in this world there's just one race to which we all belong
This is the truth that we must face, together we are strong

One World

In terms of time it seems forever that human beings were not together
For from that place our story started we then dispersed and long were parted
So much time it seems then passed that when again we met at last
It wasn't with familiar faces, our features now of different races
For this alone we should not care, but when the gun would meet the spear
It's then the power we chose to chase and through this power some chosen race
A time of conquest ever faster, as though a race to be the master
This dangerous world of disarray, where brutal force will have its sway
Yet some will say they long have sighted the world as one with all untied
And this new world to set the stage for peace and love in a prosperous age
All beings unique is a wonderous story, and one of faith and hope and glory
But though unique we share the heart to wish us close and not to part
This earnest hope to be united, our hearts the same and not divided
To be as one shall be our cause for which we'll never cease or pause

Paths To War

On paths of war they will not pause and care not for the pain they cause
Yet seem surprised as then they find, to kill cannot not win hearts and minds
When leaders seem so sure and willing to stay the course and keep on killing
Of lives being lost and goodwill spent, no time to thoughts of care is lent
This horror real and long remembered, loved ones dead, defiled, dismembered
Their memory now to be avenged through red-hot rage or cold revenge
With open eyes is how we see that war is now an industry
No righteous cause or faith in God, war for their factories and for jobs
An end to desperate poverty, the only war some wish to see
No more where wars of disrepute leave victims and the destitute
No riches spent on cruel destruction, but bridges built by care's construction
No more to see the weakened weep, to God this promise we should keep
That wars that bring such harm we're seeing to all our fellow human beings
Shall not be those cruel paths we take, it's paths to peace that we shall make

Peace Is Ours To Make

A belligerent and aggressive stance, distrust we find is fostering
It seems we're in some deadly dance with all this dangerous posturing
Childlike tantrums like a tot, and lost is moral compass
So deadly if their play then stops, much more than romp and rumpus
We bring ourselves to the brink of war, with weapons of destruction
Immerse ourselves in hurt and sore with sorrow our construction
Behaviours callous and uncouth, we must now rise above
For is it not the simple truth, we're most in need of love
It's love to which we all belong, despair we should forsake
For it's this love that keeps us strong when life seems what's at stake
No fear to feel, through care we shine, no clouds to dim the light
When love appears so sweet and fine distrust will fade from sight
To be as one and speak of love, no toll to pay or take
No more these hawks, please bring the dove, for peace is ours to make

Race

Why is race the word we use, how can it be this term we choose
As though a race shall best describe some people from a vast great tribe
To most a race is there to win, to finish first you must begin
Some race to reach an early grave, the race for freedom when once a slave
We see a race has many forms and all these races have their norms
To win the race being at the core, the race to arms that starts a war
But brutal war is mortal sin with senseless waste being what you win
And you'll be cursed for evermore if you make race the cause for war
A conflict of the human race is paradise lost being what we chase
We strive, or steal, or spend, or store, but seek what once we had before
Some difference in this life we chase, but with each other this has no place
When unity is the thing that's seen we share the visions of our dreams
It's time to know the truth we face, as one we are the human race
That we alone can take this name, and with it we are all the same

Resilience

When trouble's there to steal your light, paths once well-lit seem far from bright
Whatever now may come your way, from cold dark night comes light-filled day
Those hard-felt blows met with resilience, our human nature in all its brilliance
When though being weak, a strength we find, it's then our nature truly shines
How we'll ignore those stories told, the ones they tell to make you bold
That strength and power can come through hate, of others we should subjugate
For haters have within their soul a darkness that creates a hole
An emptiness that leaves a void, the good within we see destroyed
Their hearts seem set as hard as stone, they're in a group but all alone
For no one else will they have care, their disregard will strip them bare
Of vulnerability they have contempt, to kindness little thought is lent
They cannot see a strength in meekness, and this contributes to their weakness
From meekness true resilience blooms, dismissing all their talk of doom
It's there the truth of strength now lies, where good will grow when hatred dies

Retribution

Harsh truth that you may come to find as you face destitution
No care to call on in their minds, just violent retribution
Yet all great retribution gains are voids so deep and hollow
These paths of war bring hurt and pain that none should wish to follow
To ask who caused such dread and sore, the answer's much the same
It's they who brought such frightful war, the others are to blame
No care or thought for innocence, no feelings for a child
As what appears to now make sense, a madness of the wild
With retribution now we see a wholly vicious cycle
Where nothing good will come to be, all thoughts of care being stifled
How can these thoughts be re-arranged to peaceful ways of living
For some it seems it's just too strange to ever have forgiving
But of forgiving we must try before it's all too late
No more of war where children die, it's peace we need to make

Talk Of Slaves

You think of yourselves as so civilised, while the values of others you completely despise
And how with your history is a need to inscribe great conquests of savage and barbaric tribes
But might and great power can never be regal when flocking with crows and demeaning the eagle
Deceptive in nature you destroy and divide, while seeking for seizure all those who will hide
You trample and tear and will treat as sedition, all forms of expression from our oral tradition
Crushed are the customs that created our cultures, to wreck and to burn then to leave for your vultures
No more are we tribes or small intimate clans, no more a strong woman, now less than a man
No longer a people of that it is certain, to you we are nothing but beasts there to burden
A dreadful foreboding on tormented seas, like livestock to market we are sent where you please
To a short brutal life it is now we are bound, a cargo of tears where no love will be found
A ruthless reality to which we must yield, reduced now to slaves used for building or field
Downtrodden and beaten with the whip and the lash, our tortured existence to be turned into cash
For all of the turmoil, and all of the pain, for a life that's now shackled and struck down in chains
For the anger and sadness, and the shame that is felt, gods curse on you Roman, from we who are Celt

Teachers

To teach that special mindset sought, sometimes we then shall see
When what's being taught is full of fraught an anxiousness will be
When teachers bring a taint of hate, dismissiveness, or loathing
In some young minds this plants a stake, a sense of fear's foreboding
For this is all that hatred drives, an end and not beginning
A hatred's end for which to strive is surely full of sinning
Especially when you wish to bend the will of those so young
As though on you they can't depend, when fairness will be shunned
You put on youth your false-held truth that's caused you such frustration
It's you who now seems so uncouth with deep discrimination
And all your lies we should despise, that give to you such surety
For well we know within our lives deceit brings insecurity
When it's a poison you pass on through all that you will teach
No way for this to make you strong, true strength being out of reach

The Cult

Real power it takes a lonely seat, filled by those who are deemed elite
But evil waits there to erupt, for lonely power will then corrupt
With this the power is autocratic, opposed to all that's democratic
When power displayed seems without fault a crude charisma creates a cult
And through this cult it's then they'll state their message that is filled with hate
For those they see as not the same, as always they're the ones to blame
This cult creates a powerful vision and one that's based on deep division
An evil in their minds resides for all those now not on their side
And with these thoughts it's then they fuel a hatred that is vile and cruel
This cult has now become a force set on some brutal deadly course
When culture is being based on hate then cruel contempt will fill your plate
No food for thought with wine's sweet cup, this culture it will eat you up
From all of this we'll rise above when we embrace the gift of love
The care and kindness love can show, deflecting all their hate-filled blows

The Fighters

A troubled world is what they sight and yet for love some say they fight
For the love of God an answered call, for the love of country, and patriots all
Yet each believe they hold the right and to attack bring all their might
Bound and swayed until they fall into that dark and deathly pall
With brutal acts and mortal sins the merciless killing time begins
The screaming slaughter of a child, the wailing with emotions wild
Torn and taken by this thing of dread, now gone forever to join the dead
How do you face that fateful day when conflict's pain is due to pay
With souls that seem as dark as night, there's some that say come join the fight
They try so hard to sanitize this terror that we should despise
But there are no means to justify these vicious, murderous ways to die
For there is no winner in this cruel fight, there is no glory, power, or might
When all that truly can be managed is to be the side that is less damaged
Then the only victory to achieve is to be the one with less to grieve

The Jester

To rage against that solid wall, the one that has no gate
With stone you laid it stands so tall, your mind being filled with hate
Constructed by your wish to blame, no thoughts of love or giving
Your hatred that will have no shame for different ways of living
Their words at first were smooth as silk to trap you in their cage
To stand with others of your ilk, to channel all your rage
Their speech being used it now emboldens a discourse of contempt
And to this speech you seem beholden, no thoughts to care being lent
Some said your leader seemed a fool as though to play the jester
But all these antics were a tool, division now to fester
To bring a lie to what is true, with truth to be a lie
Distrust is what this gives to you, to faith you say goodbye
It's you who now will play the fool when you bring all your rage
The jester then breaks all the rules and struts upon the stage

True Strength

Who now knows what there has been, or where some change should start
What's real or now is just a dream, when trust seems ripped apart
In groups of states we seem so lost, some countries torn asunder
We war with little thought of cost, while rockets roll like thunder
We all should strive to be as one, and yet be individual
Distinctness we shall never shun, uniqueness being residual
A path unknown is where we walk, with courage and misgiving
But when of this we choose to talk it's then we give to living
For when we speak of strength and fear it's of ourselves we're true
When truth is what you wish to share then courage comes to you
True strength is not to be above, of others to put down
True strength is when we know of love, a smile and not a frown
It's as a group that we belong, no more to be apart
Together is where we are strong, this truth from where we start

Wars

When wealth's bestowed through family trees there forms some powerful
    dynasties
And on our lives they'll take a toll when they will strive for full control
To conquer us they'll then divide, with sanctuary some simplistic side
But in the end you're on your own, your struggle now being faced alone
What we create they make redundant as wasteful use is what's abundant
And when this waste must be resourced, it's then to war they'll steer a course
With conscience clear they'll fear no sin and make this time of dread begin
No more the talk of mending fences, it's now the killing time commences
Fuelled with fears and inflamed dangers we end the lives of total strangers
Our sights are set on who to kill, not empty stomachs we need to fill
In corrupted times we'll never see an end to wars and poverty
While wars are not what most solicit, when silent we are all complicit
It's not the meek who'll take the stage so do not fear your pent-up rage
And offer up what you can give, to change the way in which we live

Wars For Wealth And Power

There's only one true shining light and that's the light of love
The hawk again we shall not sight when we release the dove
The dove's the one to bring us peace, with hawks we're full of fears
And all these wars they then shall cease, no more to shed sad tears
The only war that we should make is one that sets us free
And when ourselves we shan't forsake, the truth of this we'll see
It's evil we can seem to face, against the human being
And if the cause of war is race, the devil we are seeing
For wealth and power they'll also war, your weakness they despise
No care to cause such hurt and sore, they're deaf to all our cries
When war is for a wealth and power there's few who'll see the gain
Through the terror they will make you cower and all we feel is pain
Be just and true towards each other, and always to yourself
War rips the heart out of a mother and rots the power of wealth

A Time To Share

Those with real power who control the community, never being poor with their wealth their immunity
Yet they show a disinterest that seems to reflect to those who know poverty they have little respect
For little is what they will choose to distribute to people who are desperate or cannot contribute
But why should they give any meaningful share when the truth of it all is they don't really care
They're quick to attack if there's mention of plenty and make their defence that the issue is envy
As though they're afraid of this talk of the poor and unpleasant truths being brought to their door
When these are the issues that they choose to ignore then more so these issues will come to the fore
When the problems of poverty will not be embraced then our civil society becomes failed and debased
Ignoring these problems can seem without sense as a caring community then becomes a pretence
Real change being the thing that they just will not try, a caring community being a cold callous lie
With the wealth we may make seeming ever abundant should the notion of scarceness not then be redundant
But embracing this concept is the thing that they fear for the system is built on strict limits of share
But fear should be focused on what limits will reap, with extremes in conditions then the outlook is bleak
For a great inequality cannot be condoned and what some can see they will wish overthrown

Automation

On a base they will sit with components that gleam, a vastness of power in cold, sterile machines

And when there are tasks that are not automated it seems that the process is slow and sedated

As a way to produce they'll relentlessly serve, more so than those made of flesh, bone, and nerves

For people get weary and some can seem lazy, but not needing people is a system that's crazy

When it's only machines that can work without pause, despair and disruption are what this can cause

Compared to machines there's a contract that's loose when we're seen as burdens and of little use

Struck off and struck down as though hit with a mallet, they shatter your dreams as your future they sell it

But what is the need for machines to produce if few can then purchase what they make for use

For lacking in money what then can you buy and the products they make stay on shelves where they lie

An ordered society could soon seem to be failing when full automation is so ever prevailing

What is this future automation is hatching, will our tasks be reduced to a form of back-scratching

Should now we be fearing a future that's looming where our only tasks seem to be each other's grooming

The purpose of work is for money to earn yet for meaningful purpose is what we all yearn

With full automation is it time now for stating, there are new ways of living we should be creating

Communists And Fascists

One says their state's for humankind, the other has a different mind
But full control both states will take, small choice for you and me to make
Of difference they will see it smothered, one state for all and not for others
From different thoughts both states have turned, of books for bonfires both
    have burned
To see themselves the master race, a power that fascists always chase
With all the rest to be as slaves, it's this their evil doctrine craves
To be as one being all the same, exclusion with no thought of shame
They'll play upon a close-held fear that not enough is there to share
Of others they will show their hatred, and how they should be subjugated
Of fascists we have had our fill and wish their ranting mouths were still
Yet communists cannot be free, their hatred is more hard to see
Of lesser evil they will show, their malice more some secret blow
When fears we have are of each other, no common ground can we discover
With both these states it will be found, extremes are at their heart unsound

Corrupted Power

The journey's end being how to lose, a path that none would choose to use
The outcome now to deal with pain when lost is all that you have gained
Yet few can stop to count the cost of what it is that they have lost
When those who seek a power so grand shall crush your will to make their stand
They crave a power through strength and might that leaves them with a blinded sight
Corrupted power for which they thirst, it seems they try to be the worst
The platform sought being just a stage to make their mark on history's page
The role they play to rant and rave, and care not how they now behave
Ignoring truth, what's wrong or right, for war they feel a love to fight
Vicious deeds to fuel their vanity as they inflict some vile insanity
And all such rampant ego shows is how what's good is laid so low
Cruel power they treat as just a tool, to hammer down a ruthless rule
As though by keeping others down, through this they wear some dreadful crown
A tyrant who will have no care for those with lives now lived in fear

Defiance

Strong winds of change now far from slow, this pace of change can leave you low
Sometimes so fast you feel the blow, your feelings you try not to show
A change where they increase their wealth is one that's swift but quiet with stealth
As though to care's left on the shelf, which makes its mark on mental health
And it's this change that they will say, for you is now the only way
If where you are you wish to stay, embrace the changed and brand-new day
They seem to thirst for full control, to take back all that giving stole
It seems you're in some deep dark hole in which they'd gladly steal your soul
No matter how they plant their stake, our souls they'll find they cannot take
As what's agreed is always fake, of us some slaves they shall not make
It's to the light that we must run, to feel the brilliance of the sun
To know again how we are one and all their darkness we will shun
For when they do as tyrants dare, and show for us they have no care
Much more than just a defiant stare is what they'll reap from lack of share

Full Control

They'll focus on the negativity and usher in some new reality
To make us fear or to despise, as though through them we shall be wise
They'll feel their false held righteous might which brings with it the will to fight
Yet those who have such self-belief create a world of pain and grief
On evil thrones sits full control, from those in power who've lost their soul
To bring the fight, they'll then proclaim, to war and kill is not insane
But if we feel we're higher beings, what of the killing that we're seeing
Is this to be what makes us proud, to end some lives then shout out loud
Their warfare we can ill afford, of life we need to have accord
To live our lives as though as one and then to see what we become
Of their control we have no need, as what this grows is toxic weed
To smother all that's right and true and have no care for me or you
So I'll believe when others say that there must be another way
For full control, that none should dare, as all it brings is deep despair

Futures

The paths we chose through time would lead us, to where we share and prosper
Where food for thought could also feed us, relationships to foster
But when there's little care or contact, nor sharing in our toil
Then we ignore the social contract and what we make is spoiled
For now we're seeing such rampant greed, of opulence being stated
No care for those in desperate need, the world seems full of hatred
With nothing here now to believe, no thing that makes you strong
No way in which we all achieve, no sense that we belong
When leaders they will show to us, it's of themselves they care
Then all their selfishness now does is strip the cupboards bare
So little seeming good and pure, no beacon full of light
The only thing of which we're sure, displays of power and might
The loss we feel when more they steal, there's little hope we hold
The only thing we see as real, our futures have been sold

Greed

To find the thought we share the globe is far too deep for some to probe
For sharing is a thing unseen, such thoughts not worthy of a dream
But of this world to share we must and not for greed to have such lust
For what's achieved by wanton greed is stripping bare all those in need
When people seem of little use neglect can then become abuse
With some who fear we'll soon be seeing more deprivation of human beings
Machines to mimic or mass produce, manipulating more need for use
These systems fully automatic that complement the autocratic
A strength of wealth that then can lead to power no longer shared but seized
By those who sit on higher seats and judge themselves to be elite
It's these elites who crave for more and cause the want that chokes the poor
They feel the greed within their core, they speak with drones and turn to war
But all our futures we will burn if on ourselves again we turn
When care's the thing that has been lost there's few who will not bear the cost

Health And Wealth

To depths so deep there's some who'll delve, to win the race and prove themselves
So they may reach their full potential, for them a contest seems essential
With strength of purpose they'll strive to gain, for those who lose they have disdain
But lives being lived for wealth and power, sense less the beauty of a flower
To judge yourself by the wealth of others has little worth in the lives of lovers
And as for time spent in the sun, well that will come when the race is won
Perhaps by then being short of breath, having run themselves to an early death
When life it seems has done its dash what matters then what they had stashed
For when they face that long dark sleep and for their lives they then could weep
What are the things that they can keep if in the ground they're buried deep
Pursuing things that make life fuller, or doing deals to chase the moolah
Yet who'll be missed, the one with money, or one whose soul's as sweet as honey
So many paths to happiness and some may find paths paved with less
When on these paths you then may choose, real wealth's the time that's yours to use

Leaders

Through all of the ages we've felt a great need for those who have strength and a courage to lead

But when it's our leaders that are seeming perverse it's then that this need is becoming our curse

Gifts and donations being deemed without malice, so strong is the taste from a sweet, poisoned chalice

Fermented contention yet gladly they'll sup it and stifle all choice by being strung like a puppet

Powerful speeches for assaulting your ears with radical statements for inflaming your fears

To be without shame but with might on their side, so thirsty for power that they cruelly divide

Pledges then given to right all that's wrong, the message delivered is to them we should throng

A pitch that proclaims them to be the great saviour when really self-interest is the thing that they favour

A wealth and a privilege to feather their nest, and for those who are close but then not for the rest

With all of their lies it's the truth they corrupt, and a storm of dissent and pure rage can erupt

Small wonder it's now these leaders we spurn, from impotent power and false promise we turn

For what in this world is the difference they make, it's not what they give but how much they can take

True leaders it seems can no longer exist, no principles used where they guide and assist

When all the disputes and debates there have been can seem as controlled by a power that's unseen

No Freedom Borrowed

When you are poor without a cent, small freedom's sought through money lent
But freedom's something you can't borrow, when taken back it brings you sorrow
The sweetest deals can soon turn sour when those who lent display their power
It's with this power they take control, to freedom then they'll take their toll
Some come to know a hard-learned lesson that what you have in your possession
Is not the thing that makes you free, much more than this shall freedom be
The truth of freedom then they'll sight, no token gift but now a right
The freedom of the democratic, opposing all that's autocratic
The right to seek and speak free thought, a struggle that can be hard-fought
And what free thought will mean to you, how it can change the things you do
The freedom of a faith in God, the freedom where you work a job
The freedom of your love to give and your free choice in how you live
The freedom to explore your mind and places there that you may find
Of our true selves we then may learn when freedom's beacon brightly burns

Power

With morals we can seem so lax when those with wealth pay little tax
Yet burdens on the poor are placed which they cannot afford to face
But those with power who seek a might care little for a weakling's plight
For this is how the poor are viewed, though not expressed in terms so crude
Their wealth is what sets them apart, this wealth the keeper of their heart
With wealth the power that lets them buy the choice for them to cheat and lie
They say it's just the way of life, that history's page is filled with strife
And if this power they will not chase, another soon shall take their place
When care's replaced by rank abuse, of power there is no truth of use
With reckless power their paths are paved, while some are used as though
    as slaves
These muted slaves of stifled choice are powerless people that have no voice
Corrupted power so tightly curled sees slavery in this modern world
This brutal power that takes its toll and on our lives has such control
The use of power should be for good, when will we see this understood

Structures

When pillars seem they're made of sand, with weight a heavy burden
No structure built on this will stand, collapse the thing that's certain
Foundation gives a structure strength, of this we are agreed
Whatever height or measured length, foundation's what you need
Of structures it's this truth we see, how strong must be the base
With people some can't see this key, from this they turn their face
That some will start from disadvantage, of this they do not care
There's even those who'll take advantage and strip them further bare
These others whom they then will mock, for pittance as they scramble
But base for them was not of rock, but more some dreadful shambles
And then to blame them for their weakness, no mood in them to fight
A lack of light that brings them bleakness, no goals to set their sight
They'll speak to them of struggle's stories, of how they've made so good
And paint their path as paved in glories, their ego understood

The Muddle

Some in this world are so filled with greed that gladly they'll take from those most in need
And that which the others just cannot afford has its value increased and is highly adored
They blatantly share their disinterest of care and thrive in a world that's so vastly unfair
They'll take up a cause for serving their vanity but seldom will have real concern for humanity
To think of themselves must always come first, with wealth being to them an unquenchable thirst
They'll pursue any course for the bountiful life and never admit to causing discord and strife
They smugly proclaim how they're full of success and never admit they exploit to excess
Some say it's this greed that has led them astray, from paths where there's sharing and a spiritual way
While others will call for a bold revolution, this seen to them as the simplest solution
From seeds of revolt what will flourish and grow, are new forms of power to lay everyone low
With none of these things do I fully agree, and some sort of muddle is all that I see
With safe middle ground being so hard to find there seems no solution for this muddled mind
While stifling my feelings of angst and despair, it's with some confusion that I then declare
The wealth that I see is so bound up with greed, some kinder investment is now what I need

The Players

The world we see before our eyes, as though it's love some now despise
A wickedness that's to the fore, of this we want to see no more
To wish for love by which to heal, but love's the thing they seem to steal
They weave their lies and state them answers, false tunes to which the cheater dances
Their egos that they hug and preen, disgrace now being the thing that's seen
With some who fumble as they fawn, allowing spite-filled cults to dawn
These players act for history's page and strut upon their strife-torn stage
With only menace on their mind and power the grip by which they bind
It's with this power they'll rant and rage, of freedom then to make a cage
Of truth to choose as just a ruse to bend or change and then to use
They care not for a deadly toll, the price that's paid for full control
For they shall never bear the cost, with them we see all justice lost
With hope we wish to rise above and find bestowed is truth and love
That of this troubled world we're seeing there is and always higher being

The Red Flag

When greed has had its evolution it's overthrown by revolution
If living free has been abused our freedoms then we all will lose
And then we'll see how they oppress, more people to be left with less
With wealth and power being autocratic, to turn against the democratic
To keep the red flag flying here are words we do not wish to hear
If wealth is what we will not share this flag may see us all stripped bare
Until such time that people rise, oppressors then to be despised
Such strength to feel at their control, but this will take a deadly toll
For throughout history we've been shown that when a power is overthrown
Another then will fill the void to take the power which they destroyed
When in our lives we do not share for others we will cease to care
What this will foster is our fear, to fight it's then that some shall dare
To take, to steal, or to abuse, is not the freedom we should choose
If freedom is the thing we cherish we must not let our freedoms perish

Troubled Youth

Some wish to fight with all their might this rank injustice that they sight
A world that's scarred by septic sores being torn by greed and constant wars
And how they feel they cannot heal, for trust is what these crimes will steal
It's answers that their minds now crave, who are these kings that made us slaves
They disobey and misbehave, and then they'll choose to rant and rave
As disrespectful they're portrayed, the change they seek once more delayed
They call them crazed and troubled youth, but what they wish for is the truth
For all these wounds upon their futures, are seeming stitched with barbed-wire sutures
These lies are lesions to their soul, as legions then they'll take control
Of those harsh streets that have no care, in desperate times they have no fear
For those with power have ill repute and seem to wish them destitute
Corrupted kings that have no crown, who use their might to tear them down
There is no future they can see, no path with hope to set them free
So arm in arm and hand in hand this troubled youth will make their stand

Unbalanced

Complexity that dims the light and leaves you with some blinded sight
Can take its toll upon your mind, confusion being the thing you find
Simplicity they say is pure, of this it seems you're not so sure
As simple is the way some state their message that is full of hate
Considered is how things should be, and laced with truths for all to see
For when your cause is filled with lies your speech is what becomes despised
And then it's with complete distrust, to view you others feel they must
But now some seem to stoke the rage, so they will find they've gained the stage
Expressing rage is what they wish, the fruit that fills their poisoned dish
To feed the discord and the strife that seems a plague on modern life
Their rhetoric that we see being used that leads to others being abused
Leaves nothing but some cold contempt, when goodwill has been lost or spent
To wish to take another's side should not be seen as to divide
Societies where all must agree are not the ones where we are free

Values

When lacking faith there's disconnect, no soul to shield or to protect
With life being lived as though it's seeming, devoid of purpose and of meaning
The value for which some will strive being that where ego strokes their pride
When this will make them feel alive it's to themselves we know they've lied
For there's a truth you often find that those with ego on their mind
Make measure of their mental health, dependent on displays of wealth
To share to them is seen as wrong, of others they do not belong
It's then they'll know a life that's spent in cruel yet casual, cold contempt
When scruples lie thin on the ground their actions soon can seem unsound
As all the choices that they make depend on what they now can take
Yet some will have a different view, to care for others being what they do
To nurse the sick or fight a fire, to be of help their true desire
But valued less in what they're paid is how we see this truth displayed
For value seems not what we need, but only that which stems from greed

The Human Condition

Abuse

Abuse you find plays on your mind, into the depths it seeps
When others are being cruel not kind from you there's not a peep
For with cruel words they cut a swathe that wounds down to your soul
As though in torment you should bathe, to feel now less than whole
But it's with kindness they first came, they spoke with words of love
Yet now they wish to cause you pain, they swear and push and shove
A change in them that takes control, this change to you seems massive
Submissive seems to be your role as you become so passive
But they're the ones who're truly weak, being vicious is not strong
And those cruel words with which they speak, to you do not belong
Don't listen now to what they say, these words you should not hear
It's time to live a different way and for yourself have care
So turn from all the hurt that's hurled, from this you'll rise above
For you are special in this world, deserving of true love

Actors

Some stand upon the actor's stage, it's been this way through every age
There to express our human story, of tragedy and tales of glory
Emotions that we strongly feel, the actor plays to make it real
The beauty of a loving soul, how when love comes it makes us whole
Of depths of darkness and despair, of feeling bright and light as air
Or of a mind with thoughts entwined, manipulation so refined
Of those who ever now seem dreaming of ways and means of subtle scheming
A smouldering sense of pent-up rage when caught as though trapped in a cage
Someone who has a mind to kill, to play this is the actor's skill
Of tales where torment feels like hell, it's these and more the actor tells
How greed shall always plant the seed of little care for those in need
Of how we differ is overrated by those who wish us separated
Where tribulations from the start are overcome through strength of heart
Of all of this will actors show, we watch the play and come to know

Ancient Greeks

On seas their sleek-lined ships would sail, they skimmed upon the surface
Beneath the waves of gods to hail, protection being the purpose
It's in their minds these thoughts would play of gods and monstrous beings
With deep blue seas and sacred days, their gods to them all-seeing
To sail their ships to unknown shores and give thanks to Poseidon
Through reverence is how they ensured their gods were there beside them
On charted seas to ply their trade and overcome privation
And then to find that they have made from outposts now a nation
To take their place upon the stage with Zeus and armoured heroes
Of volumes filled with history's page, to conquer mighty pharaohs
Of plays and of philosophy, of old ways they would rupture
To give the world democracy and art that gleams with lustre
What they would bring into the world, a classical perfection
With their embrace being tightly curled on freedoms for protection

Betrayal

Malicious minds can seem so keen to see the end of hopes and dreams
With spiteful words they say you fail, and in your heart there lies betrayal
That in your mind are thoughts of lust and at your core you'll breach a trust
The seeker of a strong temptation as though to crave some wild elation
There's more to hear, they'll then insist, of pleasures that you can't resist
But all your deeds are overstated by those so tainted with their hatred
They'll scheme to make your home a hovel, down on your knees it's then
    you'll grovel
With comfort lost, trust torn and shred, cold vacant space to share your bed
And in this bed you won't rest long, no more to share for sharing's gone
With ships of fools you'll see you've sailed and feel the loss of how you've failed
You're not alone to walk this road, yet seeds of lonely times you've sowed
Such longing for those warm sweet days, to feel again those loving ways
It's now the way you wish to live is less to take and more to give
Sincere of heart shall be your path, the bridge to love being what you craft

Champion's Heart

The champion's load is never light when victory's road is in plain sight
You need to show your power and might, a strength that grows to bring the fight
Yet some don't wish the champion's fate, of challenge that brings with it weight
The simplest path the one they choose, where less to gain means less to lose
It's fear they find that holds them back, a fear of what they think they lack
The champion's path they would not seek, their fear can leave them feeling meek
Within yourself you know you're strong, that on this path you now belong
To set aside what's old and stale, it's with such thoughts you will not fail
Through this you feel the champion's heart, the end you see there from the start
Your will to make you reach your goal, what's fractured you will now make whole
To make a change, with steady hand, those lines now drawn down in the sand
Much more than just a change of pace, a changed perspective you must face
To overcome and then achieve, with this there can be no reprieve
It's then you'll find the champion's way has brought the bright and brand-new day

Colonisers

We make a life with dexterous hands and work the soil upon the land
With nature being the thing to cherish, for if destroyed then all will perish
Yet when we channel strength and will we'll move of mountain or a hill
While for this world we must be one our journeys have not yet begun
The freedom, which is that of space, this choice we'll find that's ours to chase
Remoteness where the starlight gleams is where we'll realise long-held dreams
To cross the void and still survive, it's this for which we now should strive
This voyage that's within our soul, its newness that makes us feel whole
To know the risk yet take the chance, on other worlds for us to dance
Of fear we need to take no heed, we'll build a life and plant our seed
To feel with all that we are one beneath some moon or bright-lit sun
These suns that turn the deep cold warm, the light from stars where life
    can swarm
Like pinpricks to a darkened stage these shining stars that make an age
To venture out will make us strong for it's in space that we belong

Come Together

In civil times there's never been a caring age with fairness seen
No golden time of light and vision without some dark and desperate prison
Through all of time we've fought to live, yet seldom have we fought to give
No more a sister or a brother, when sights are set upon each other
Wealth that flows as though a stream, when dammed will leave just dust-filled dreams
While want that sees such desperate need lies unfulfilled through endless greed
Why is it greed that's to the fore, unnatural need crying out for more
Stark emptiness there at its core, false value then enshrined by law
Such cruelty now we need not face, this world is for the human race
For friends and family to love and cherish, without them we should surely perish
An age ago our path decided, to come together, not stay divided
With unity to make us free, this outcome then we all could see
We shall not run and cannot hide, now is the time we must decide
To be as one and come together, to love each other more than ever

Competition

When competition seems it's based on unforgiving daring
To some it feels it's without grace, so coarse and overbearing
They say when competition's rife much less there is for sharing
And this shall be the cause for strife, as few will show some caring
But competition's nature's way in all of our surrounds
A force which always will hold sway, in nature it abounds
The seed that floats upon the breeze to find its patch of ground
And there to lie, yet with an ease, to grow so strong and sound
As nature brings its force to bear and all of life competes
There's nothing else that can compare, it's nature that completes
Those lovely things that nature brings, through great and wondrous feats
Of forests full of birds that sing, of all of nature's treats
With competition things will thrive, it's this that makes them strong
Through competition we've arrived, in this we all belong

Competitor

Everything is in your mood, to smile and sing, or weep and brood
Your mood defining how you see whatever challenge there may be
The challenge that you now must face, your choice to win or lose the race
The feeling that you have inside, will make you fight or run and hide
But it's your heart that makes you strong, it puts your mind where you belong
To find the true depths of your soul and bring to you what makes you whole
It's courage now that you require, a courage burning deep with fire
To persevere and win this fight, what's heavy must be seen as light
Against yourself the fight's now cast, to win or lose is to outlast
With no reprieve and no relief, it's then you need your self-belief
To feel as though a hungry predator and not some weak or stale competitor
But the hunter that seeks out the game, to win that victory's prize and fame
It's all your strength that you must use to win this fight and not to lose
The sweetest victory you shall sight, when from within you bring your might

Country Girl

From Queensland came a country girl, her beauty more than pretty
She thought she'd give it all a whirl and headed for the city
A stable place, a source of strength, for this she had a hunger
And though the time seemed long in length, she couldn't be much younger
When citybound it's then she found, how life is full of layers
How hard to find that solid ground surrounded by some players
She came to know that solid ground must be of her creation
Within herself be strong and sound, this strength to give foundation
But with this strength there was not lost, that caring, loving feeling
For that's a strength with too much cost which can't allow for healing
A healing way being on display, sometimes through confrontation
And then with tender, gentler ways and calm co-operation
At times she finds she doubts her skill and has a vulnerability
But well you know she has the will, and more so the ability

Dancing

Dancing to the rhythm's beat, so cool when you can feel the heat
And how the moves just seem to flow when joy is what we gladly show
So dance on to the morning light, when dawn's soft glow is turning bright
It's there you'll find in your mind's sight, the weight of burdens seeming light
This dancing that's within our souls that takes us back where we feel whole
To bring the joy that staleness stole, where movement is our only role
To feel so drawn to shake and move, and now in need to find the groove
As though surrendered to the rhythm, from seriousness the sweetest schism
We dance so strong to favourite songs, the ones we know where joy belongs
And it's this joy we wish to share, to show how much we love and care
Of dancing we will never tire, to whirl in halls, around rings of fire
To dance is when we truly make the time we need to celebrate
To twirl can put some in a trance where choice will join with games of chance
You find your feelings are enhanced when you embrace the gift of dance

Deception

You know that what you see is real, no matter what they say
You know the truth of what you feel, of how this is the way
For what we see before our eyes, in this we must believe
All else is then just more of lies, by which they will deceive
They say theirs is the cause of right, yet strongly have they lied
A vision full of might they sight, and all is justified
Yet others can promote deception through their misunderstanding
Distorted views form their perception, belief becomes demanding
That all shall see a truth so pure, their doctrines seen as virtue
Of this you're clearly not so sure, when doctrines seem to hurt you
A truth can only shine and glisten when you will know its way
To know, it's first that you must listen, let others have their say
And then to take in conversation of what may be agreed
An openness with consultation, no more to be deceived

Dog

Three letters used like that of god, these letters being the same
It's not of ant or ass or hog, it's dog that takes this name
A mirrored image of letters used, so different is the meaning
And some can state they seem amused of how this use is seeming
For dog is not of righteousness, of glory from above
Yet dogs have certain consciousness, we feel they know our love
A dog cannot have thoughtfulness, compassion for the weak
Companionship with gentleness, with dogs it's this some seek
A dog is not an unseen force for what's deemed right and true
But dogs at times can be the source that brings some joy to you
True power these dogs cannot display, make measure of your soul
But dogs it seems can have their way to make some days feel good and whole
So of these words three letters state, such difference in their meaning
And how these words to each can state a truth that brings some meaning

Egomaniac

Through ego is how you may find your driver of success
Yet too much ego on your mind creates a crude excess
No balance sought when ego-driven, achievements overrated
No equal measure has been given, with worth being overstated
When ego is the thing being seen it seems that you expect
Your ego others then should preen, acknowledge their respect
No point in being realistic, for you this does not matter
As when you seem so narcissistic their talk is just some chatter
And soon we find what you've created to fill up your surrounds
To feed your need to feel as feted, false praise that now abounds
A fantasy in which you're lost where you must be the hero
It's others who must count the cost, what's gained seems close to zero
It's been more than just some short while since we have come to know
There's little substance and no style in that of which you show

Failure

Those times you feel you cannot win, it's then you'll wish for toughened skin
Shell hardened like an armadillo, yet solace sought through comfort's pillow
A shell in which you'll now reside, your skin to then become your hide
You seem caught up in failure's cage with anger that's devoid of rage
To test yourself the thing you'll shun, of challenge you now feel you're done
To shy away being like an ointment that calms and soothes your disappointment
It's in this place you feel you'll stay, no need to now re-join the play
Nor walk again upon the stage, or turn once more another page
But this is folly for a fool who can't see loss as but a tool
A way to learn from past mistakes and know full well just what it takes
Of failure when you've had your fill no longer can it make you still
Achievement is what you desire, it's this that sets your heart on fire
Success depends on state of mind so with yourself be true and kind
With all the things that you have learned it's failure that you'll find has turned

Families

Family there to make you strong, to feel that you're belonging
How much you miss them when you're gone, a strength that's now of longing
For it's with family we connect, that special way of living
Of family how we will protect, of fights and of forgiving
A sense of family for which we thirst, no second best being rendered
As family always will come first, to care is what's being tendered
For in a family you're the same but share your different feelings
Those times you share more than a name, through family there is healing
A love that leaves you calm and still, a sense of where you're grounded
And how to most this brings a will, new families to be founded
Extended family like some clan, a tribe that forms relations
Which seems to follow its own plan with sorrows and elations
It's for our families we will cheer and feel them close at heart
Our need for which we hold so dear, our wish being not to part

Forty-Two

From twenty-one to forty-two, some shortened time this seems to you
To reach the age of twenty-one, long seemed the days spent in the sun
No matter now how much you try the days and weeks, and months fly by
As though your life is now a race, no more that calm and slower pace
Your hope that when this race will end it's then you'll have some time to spend
Relaxing in the sun's warm rays, such tranquil, calm, and serene days
Yet still they want you to believe the race is where you will achieve
And to the race when all you give, brings meaning to the life you live
They care not for the toll this takes but only for how much this makes
For profit and for wealth to gain, for this there needs to be some pain
But memories of the life we made are all that really can be saved
A life with love, good cheer, and health, it's this that truly is our wealth
So do not live your life in haste as then it seems your time you waste
And none should ever have the will to rush and never to be still

Full Circle

Look at that dog and the joy it will bring, the birds in free flight and the way that they sing
The cat that's so lazy it seems without care, while the lives that we live just cannot compare
Creatures so free there to live for the moment, but a similar freedom some cannot condone it
For they live a life that is set for achieving, attaining the goals that will give their lives meaning
They constantly wrestle and struggle with stress, to be those with more and not one with less
To handle the pressure they'll disregard health, as far more important is their status and wealth
Our life is our time, but we don't seem to own it, to relax and reflect seems so small a component
With time being measured, recorded in logs, some wish for the freedom of the cats and the dogs
Perhaps in the future it is then we shall see that time has no cost as it's been made free
No need to juggle with time that is rated, a pressure released, and a tension sedated
Some golden age for which we can dream, with power being abundant yet burning so clean
Where waters run clear, with fragrant fresh air, and lives can be lived without worry or fear
A time for each other and a time full of caring, again in the future a wealth full of sharing
Through changes to living we're seeming to hurtle, perhaps what we'll see is we've come a full circle

Gangs

When we were young with each other we'd hang, laugh at the joke when we named our own gang
But as we got older real gangs we would find, could bring a brutality that can mess with your mind
To walk through those doors, breeze in like a charm, no thoughts in our heads there could ever harm
Like a trio of bandits they then stormed up the stairs, destroying our fun to bring cold, crushing fears
And now more than ever your nerves are unsteady, when in front of your face is being waved a machete
Sawn off at the barrel with a shortened gun stock, when placed at your head this will put you in shock
An axe being swung with a shout and a grunt, though not with the sharp end but the one that is blunt
Their wish to bring terror, so they can be feared, a lack of compassion when it's death to be dared
To stand to your ground or to quickly now run, no easy choice when you're feeling so stunned
To bash and to batter both body and psyche, these are the ways of a cruel, vicious bikie
To push to the gutter, down into the dirt, the purpose of gangs is intent to cause hurt
What's in their way they will brutally hammer, while darkly promoting cruel violence has glamour
Compared to these others our gang seemed so meek, considered as no more than simply piss-weak
But with weakness our fault it was so hard to fail, as most of us managed to stay out of jail

God Of Guns

On the altar of your god of guns it's children's blood that freely runs
And all our tears become a flood when you accept sweet children's blood
This strength of faith in guns you find, entices, and excites your mind
Such innocence being sacrificed, your faith is now a god of vice
It snuffs the light and takes the breath, your god of guns that deals in death
A power so cruel and overrated, with all your rights being overstated
Who gave to you the right to choose that children die so you won't lose
The power that guns will bring to killing, with all the blood that keeps on spilling
These rights you state that must be saved, form pools of blood in which you bathe
With guns and death you're mesmerised, as though with blood you are baptised
When children's blood won't quench your thirst, we look at you and see the worst
As though a child is sacrificed, for guns you calmly pay this price
The future in some mournful hearse, your god of guns is now a curse
Sweet children that you will not save, for to your god you're now a slave

Gun Lobby

No longer protecting a pastime or hobby, this group seeks a power to convince when they lobby

Expressing the faith in their guns with a fervour, the bearing of arms has extended much further

Respectful of others is how they're portrayed, but death tolls now show there's a trust that's betrayed

And it's from this harm there can seem no relief, possession of guns being some sacred belief

As they focus their sights on the worship of guns, from mayhem and murder is how the blood runs

Being butchered by bullets on a barbaric altar, so brutally slayed, still their faith does not falter

No moves for reforms as your leaders sit still, then say that a gun's not to blame when they kill

Solutions are stymied, reform being stalled, while the murder of innocents will leave us appalled

They refuse to address ways to stem or to stifle such gut-wrenching deaths from a gun or a rifle

These weapons of war used for deadly assault, but still they will say that with guns there's no fault

The message delivered can only be blunt, these are weapons for murder and not for the hunt

A blind, brutal faith in the gun at their side, devotion so strong that from truth they will hide

This terror and slaughter of daughters and sons, maddening mass killings from the use of these guns

To refuse to agree that these weapons be banned, by ignoring these killings they are sure to be damned

Happiness

It's happiness that we pursue, no wish for hurt and pain
This light to life for me and you, contentment ours to gain
At times our lives can seem a trial when all seems such a grind
But if to this you give a smile a lighter mood you'll find
To be with friends that we hold dear, where laughter fills the air
When happy voices we will hear, it's of ourselves we share
True happiness cannot be bought, too great will be the cost
As what it is that you first sought shall soon to you be lost
For happiness where may you look, for peace of mind to find
Now in a field or by a brook, a place to ease your mind
Perhaps a beach on sunny days, or thrills that give a rush
To sit and soak in sun's sweet rays, the forest green and lush
With life there is no time to lose, its journey takes us far
Real happiness is yours to choose no matter where you are

Holidays

There is no need for negativity, I've had my fill of bleak
It's now I wish for positivity, some shining light I seek
Those thoughts to dial an untapped smile and bring a change of mind
For nothing else seems worth the while, some happiness to find
To feel in life there's now more pleasure, just waiting to be found
My mind at rest with thoughts of leisure, this feeling seems profound
And there to take in nature's sights, of all these wonderous things
A freshened air and sparkling light are what this feeling brings
So lift me up to let me breathe and smell that scented air
To make me feel that I believe, for now no need to care
Adventurous things that I can do, with this my mind to toy
And spend some time for me and you to bring us both some joy
It's in this sun-blessed state I'll stay; I have no mind to move
To love and laugh through all the day, so deep now in this groove

Homeless

A deep desperation, no place to call home, it's now that you feel you are truly alone

And of all those dreams there to share with another, a life that is full of oppression will smother

A grim realisation of what's now in store, being outcast and exiled and torn to your core

No light to your life as in darkness it's draped, and you cannot perceive of some way to escape

To crave for some comfort, a small space reserved, as though that for you this is all that's deserved

But little is found on the streets where you roam, your bed now being made on some cold and hard stone

Perhaps it was illness that seemed to have caused, a life that's despairing and so callously paused

What stolen dreams were the ones that you chased, was it cruel chance that now sees you displaced

Just how can it be that you find you've arrived, to a place where each day seems a thing to survive

When stress and anxiety can make anyone ill, this homeless existence most surely then will

Is it some kindness for which you would pray, while trying to keep desperate feelings at bay

Compassion and comfort when life seems so stark, a flicker of hope that may brighten the dark

For these homeless people we try not to see, to show them some kindness and care is the key

A future that's bleak takes a toll on your soul when the path of your plight seems beyond your control

Isolated

When in this world you seem alone cold comfort is the thing that's known
No friend or family, group, or tribe, no one to be close by your side
No company here for you to keep, these feelings that could make you weep
A desperate type of desolation now joins you in your isolation
It seems the things that once held truth lie with some long-lost hope of youth
From promise it's so far you fell to form some hollow, empty shell
You steal outside and see the sore of shameless greed that wants for more
When care's what few will give or lend, into your shell you're back again
For all you see is frightful need ignored through cruel and grasping greed
As though defiled, devoid of grace, some other world you'd rather face
This world is full of tears being cried, there's more than you who wish to hide
But none will want to take the blame and then admit to guilt and shame
You think of all the ways you've failed, feel fault for going off the rails
You're not alone with hurt and pain, there's more who've missed the gravy train

Jaded

This industrialised world to which we must give, makes demands on our time and the way we now live

A change to our living across all the nations, replacing communities with organisations

To strict codes of conduct they expect us to pledge, keep sharp as razor our competitive edge

To wield like a sword or to use as a shield, to always ensure we're the best in the field

Our weariness seems without pause or abatement, our purpose and cause in a crisp mission statement

And though it's untrue there's a feeling we must, speak well of respect and belief in a trust

Yet their statement of values seems false and pathetic, when success is achieved by ignoring an ethic

For when values and ethics are not what they own, they'll seek a diversion to appear to atone

But some are so ruthless as though without shame, and pursue with a vigour their fortune to gain

No more to give thanks in some quiet, sacred hall, false profit their idol for an upmarket mall

Whatever it takes they'll pursue all the laurels, forgoing what's right by ignoring our morals

To win at all costs by conceiving a rort, they swindle each other and sell everyone short

To trust we can see there is great degradation as they change all the rules and dilute regulation

When care and compassion are the things that are filed, a freedom of choice can become harsh and wild

Journeys

When wistful thoughts will see you pray for that for which you cannot pay
It's well you'll know the tale of wealth and how its truth is time and health
The place to which you've now arrived may not be one for which you've strived
The chapter and your story's stage aligned with timelines and with age
As days fly by like pages turned, for things familiar you then can yearn
As if it's memories that you chase, the ones etched deep upon your face
Those times that now are long since passed, how brief it was they seemed to last
No more than just a small, short while, when life felt full of beaming smiles
But when your will is strong and sound a new direction's often found
Where you may know an inner peace and times of doubt have cause to cease
To take the trails where your mind ranges, your journey is not filled with strangers
With gentle paths and lightened loads, much less of twisting, winding roads
Our journeys are the way we live, where some will take, and some will give
The journey's path we wish to find is filled with love so sweet and kind

Justice

For justice we will always wish, a truth in what will be
Instead it's just some poisoned dish, corruption's what we see
They strip away the things that matter and leave us standing bare
Their legal words are just some chatter, that shows there is no care
True justice is as sweet as honey, its purity is sound
But now it all depends on money for you to stand your ground
It's more than just some bitter frown when cut through to your core
They carve you up and put you down, so you won't ask for more
So silent is the unseen power, of which they do its bidding
From fear they wish to make you cower, of justice they are kidding
For all your words, they'll turn and twist, to give you cause to stammer
Transgressions on some pointed list, your soul to smash and hammer
So when in court they sell you short through power being on display
You know that justice is a rort, corruption being its way

Meetings

When passive cannot be your role in formal structured meetings
As there's a need for full control when tension gives its greetings
It's at these times that you may find can come a sense of doubt
Uncertain being your state of mind creates the urge to shout
And when the tension has been raised by those who hold propriety
With this it's hard to feel unfazed, in fact you feel anxiety
For those who sit within the room can seem in competition
And heightened tension quickly looms when speech is repetition
For some can seem they have no care for what the others say
They will not listen to what they hear, as they must have their way
And as you try to keep control the meeting seems to worsen
They say you should vacate the role when acting as chairperson
The thing to seek and then to find when civil discourse shatters
How you should clearly keep in mind how little all this matters

Music

This music that brings joy to hear, a tempered tone-filled beat
To sing that song it's now you'll dare, to lift you from your seat
For with this beat you can't sit still, a wish for flowing motion
Your mind now with emotions filled when music is the potion
Of all the tunes that you will hear, the strength that comes through sound
Of songs of love that conquers fear to fill up your surrounds
It seems to some an awesome feat, this rhythm formed in base
As though it is some special treat, this beat that you now chase
Percussion that can seem to boom and with it you feel whole
The beat first felt within the womb, a rhythm to your soul
But more than beat is what you'll hear with symphony of sound
These sounds as one to fill the air can then seem so profound
With music we can be so blessed in what it brings to living
Without it life can then seem less, through music we are giving

Natural Leader

That you were never meant to lead, it's doubt you find will plant this seed
But of this you must not take heed, to lead is what you want and need
You know you are a natural leader, but doubt becomes the forlorn feeder
That cancels all your positivity, to stifle growth and creativity
A natural leader has the team and feels direction where none has been
Foundation's strength from where to start, a journey with both hope and heart
For leadership you have the skills, much more than just to feel the will
But planning for the future's goals, of redefining tasks and roles
And how you know that with the team that what's important to be seen
Is fairness in how things are done, to make the team become as one
With all the challenge that you sight, you know through you this team unites
Performance more than just the deal, to care being how the deal is sealed
In this you now project a trust, to choose to care to you a must
Your goals attained anticipated, when care and trust's reciprocated

Of Ants And Antelopes

They scurry through their darkened hill, soldiers, workers, never still
The colony being their only purpose, their lives devoted to its service
The actions of an individual can never seem to be residual
For as a mass they work as one, so programmed that all else they shun
Within a herd, not roaming solitary, together grouped but not a colony
Upon the plain with sunny days and with the rain on grass to graze
No more to roam for now they're still, they graze until they've had their fill
But not for long it's there they'll stay; they move along while calves will play
Such difference with these unlike creatures, much more than just their species'
    features
The difference in the way they live, their freedom or their lives to give
In ways we live at times we're seeing a difference between human beings
Some crave a commune for us all while others preach pure freedom's call
But of extremes we have no need as there you'll find division's seed
Where conflict cannot find a nest it's from this place we'll be our best

Outrage

They set the scene upon their stage, their act to be a rant and rage
Behaviour does not suit their age when they will choose to show outrage
A bitter tone is what seems rendered, how dare you make them feel offended
Your actions cannot be defended, apologies should now be tendered
The message that they strongly send is hurt is all you seem to lend
That you can never be their friend, how they will never truly mend
With all the outrage that they state their message seems one full of hate
And how it's you that does not rate, this seems the normal way of late
But this is not the way to act, to let your feelings upstage fact
To speak with little care or tact, a brittle conversion stacked
We used to have some cordiality that had its basis in reality
But now we have some new duality and actions have no use for charity
Through outrage some can stoop so low, they reap the bitterness they sow
When just being used to strike some blow it's outrage that they should not show

Party Girl

To party on is such a thing when voices lift as though to sing
So far from ever seeming coy, as you express your love of joy
It's from those depths down to your soul, to party seems to be your role
Of dismal days they now are done, as you embrace this sense of fun
Being in a crowd that feels so close is what you now enjoy the most
It's shyness that you feel you'll shun as all the room can seem as one
No shame at all to pose and prance, this playfulness that you enhance
It's by design and not by chance, you choose to whirl, and twirl, and dance
With lights that shine so bold and bright, the spectrum's colours in your sight
The flashing movement of a strobe, the mirror ball as though a globe
And on the floor to feel a fusion, as dance becomes a sense of union
Where bodies move as they will greet this rhythm with pulsating beat
So party on and have your fill, for well you know you can't be still
The ripples now become a flow, when joy is what you wish to show

Pompeii

The earth's thin crust as though the lock that keeps reserves of molten rock
Like liquid gold to have in store, renewal erupts from earth's hot core
But this renewal comes with a cost, what's in its path can then be lost
So powerful are these great eruptions, hot ash and rock that cause destruction
With thunder crashing deep and loud, a seething pyroclastic cloud
This ash and smoke made night from day, the mountain turned and took Pompeii
A terror felt that shapes your thought when in this cauldron you've been caught
To safety's path you'll try to flee but it's too dark for you to see
Through rubble on the streets you walk, with troubled speech you try to talk
But it's your strength that's now been sapped as you can see how you've been trapped
It's clear destruction quickly looms and soon you'll greet impending doom
Approaching close so swift and fast it seems your fate has now been cast
And though now passed so many years, we still can sense your pain and fears
Together you're with those held dear, so close to nearly cause a tear

Random Nights

Some feel the need for random nights, those ones of fun and leisure
No more of mundane in their sights, for now's the time for pleasure
When they have had enough of work they feel so tired and weary
The bleakest tasks they wish to shirk, such duties seem so dreary
Of bridges over trouble spanned, and jobs to be completed
How all the answers they had planned can make them feel depleted
And how at times they feel so pained, no way to feel relieved
As turmoil seems what they have gained, it's this that they've achieved
At trouble's tasks they shouldn't stare but this becomes their action
To move they do not have a fear, it's just a lack of traction
A burnout is what they can feel, small sense to feel of winning
When others blame it's this they steal, and motion's wheels are spinning
So then they'll have their random nights, of fun being on display
For this will then put things to right, to face the brand-new day

Retreats

Of nature seen, kayaking streams, through activeness to seem so keen
A group where no one's seen as failing especially when you're now abseiling
A truthful team that now unites, forgone frustration full of fight
For from the city you seem so far, which brings you to this Kumbaya
With praises you now find accord, a grumble you can ill afford
Of closeness you must all be fond as with each other you now bond
At no time should your thoughts then stray of how you'd wish to get away
For far away is where you're at, no way to leave and that's a fact
A meeting where the news is tough as extra earnings aren't enough
But passed along is wonderous news of fees and charges there to use
Make sure how well you then will learn just how much more we all can earn
For when you've soaked up nature's glory, your team will need to know the story
Of this you know of sweet retreats with challenge that is brought through feats
It's more than just some humble hunch, free things can never come with lunch

Security

You wish a place to feel secure, where solace can be found
But comfort cannot be assured when poor are your surrounds
A place that's safe you wish to find, your struggle's laid to rest
Where there can be some peace of mind and not this life of less
For when you've nothing left to spend of this you can be sure
Your struggles seem to have no end, of problems there's no cure
When less is what life has in store and hope cannot be found
It's in this way you're truly poor, despondency abounds
A harsh reality is what you see, no rhythm you can find
No structure can there ever be but make do all the time
When fortune's not a thing that's smiled and choice is stripped away
Then life can seem so rough and wild with anger on display
You wish for what is just and fair, but this you know as true
If few will truly show they care there's little you can do

Ships of State

On seas that have a gentle breeze to wish our ships are sailing
Our future course being mapped with ease, in this we're surely failing
For now it seems that we must warn of rumblings and foreboding
How near what once were distant storms, of troubled times now loading
To voyage now can seem cut short, afloat but rudders spasm
As though to plunder how some rort, a whirlpool forms a chasm
A wreck is what we'll see will be of humbled ships of state
They slowly slip beneath the sea when greed brings fear and hate
And now some set their course to fight, of wealth to have the sources
And yet it seems within plain sight are bountiful resources
These men of war they will attack, no other course but their way
Strong winds of war to face or tack, from this there seems no leeway
As though no longer are there rules, no law to calm the sea
Some ships of state seem steered by fools, true captains they can't be

Slave Within The State

Much more than spoken words to heed, to face this frightful place
With slavery you'll pay for your deed, a brutal life you'll face
A life of cruel incarceration, a slave within the state
For you there is no sense of nation, it seems it's you they hate
With nothing now but pure survival, dysfunction you must face
And what you see is purely tribal, division based on race
A number now in common clothing, conditions being abysmal
As though for you the world has loathing, no more an individual
Coercion to create correction, some better you to make
But now you wish for insurrection, from them you want to take
For they will have you brutalised and care not what they see
To leave you scarred and traumatised, and then to set you free
No matter what it is you try the path seems old and stale
Enough to make you feel you'll cry as you're set up to fail

Spacecraft

A saucer as a spacecraft's shape, a sleek and shining sphere
Some centrifugal spin it makes to cut through atmosphere
Small are the heat shields for protection, when spinning is its surface
A spinning craft seems such perfection when space flight is its purpose
With magnetism at its core, like hubs within our wheels
Its centre's where the power is stored, the outer surface reels
Our spacecraft's at an early stage but filled with awe and wonder
When rocket fuel will burn and rage and lift off booms like thunder
It's with these craft so long and slim we journey into space
Just what it is that we begin will quickly gather pace
For space is where our future lies, new chapters there to start
It's more than spacecraft that will fly, our dreams give journeys heart
The saucer shape for outer space seems like some special seed
To find in space another place is what we truly need

Sporting Life

That we can be our best in sport, a competition without a rort
To pit ourselves against each other, a sporting chance we will not smother
For all our individual duels are bound by borders and within rules
It's there we have our equal chance, to run, to swim, to fight, to dance
And then to know the sweetest story, the one that's made from hope and glory
Where how the truth is to believe in all that waits there to achieve
As individuals or as a team, arenas filled with long-held dreams
But from beginnings never parted, these dreams from where your journey started
And what we see of sportsmanship are teams of true companionship
Commitment to a common goal where each will strive to fill their role
It's this that makes adoring fans that loudly cheer on from the stands
Where all can sense the tension rise when in plain sight is victory's prize
So shout out to this sporting life where to compete does not mean strife
And all the trials with all the pain are worth the sense of pride you gain

Suspicion

There's some who see that all decisions have with them unseen meaning
Authority viewed with such suspicion, decisions deemed demeaning
That for themselves they have a fear as they were not consulted
How no one else can seem to care, through disregard insulted
It's then they look for whom to blame, so strong is their belief
How those to blame should be ashamed for causing them this grief
And any words that may be spoken, to analyse they must
As what to them seems crushed and broken, simplicity of trust
Subconscious thought begins its leaning to paranoia's stumbling
All other's words are full of scheming, their own words full of grumbling
For what's being shown is now resented, to them it seems unfair
They disagree with what's presented, for truth they do not care
What is the way that you can deal with those of doubt-filled minds
Suspicion makes things hard to heal with kind thoughts hard to find

The Bully

You choose to demean, to put others down, take pleasure in turning a smile to a frown
It seems you are destined to have no control of a spiritual weakness etched deep in your soul
And now over time we can see how it's worsened, and how you display as a deviant person
Your heart being filled with a wish to destroy, your conceited contempt that brings others no joy
It's with a pretence you portray that you're meek, yet really it's power that you truly seek
But for you there's a terror in standing alone, with courage the thing you're unable to own
Countless are times you've cheated and lied, honesty and integrity, the things that have died
To demean and to scheme can never be pretty, but you are the one in most need of our pity
As you try to conceal all your feelings of hate, it's plain now to see that for you it's too late
No more is there doubt, for now we know fully, the ways and the means of how you will bully
How the ways to achieve all you wish to attain are used against others to inflict some more pain
Abuse full of loathing is how you're empowered, all from the mouth of a small spineless coward
So why should we care if you laugh or you sneer, when your only wish is to make us feel fear
We'll no longer listen to that which we hear, for we know the value of all we hold dear

The Drug Addiction

There are some who have a powerful need, a separate will that they must feed
That special way they wish to feel, a different view than what is real
Some small escape the thing to find, an altered state and sense of mind
A different feeling that they can choose, dependent on the drug they use
But thoughts and actions soon turn viral, when on some dreadful downward spiral
In the callous grip of a maddening drug, no sweet embrace this crushing hug
No more serenely altered states, this drug disturbs and agitates
To feel unease with skin that crawls, there is no peace when in its thrall
Yet all they sought there from the first, to quench the need for which they thirst
When all the things they feel and see, seem not for them how they should be
Their need must now be satisfied, for which they'll steal, hurt, beg, and lie
It's then this drug has full control, and on their body it takes its toll
To trust such drugs shall never take, your strength of mind, or body break
A dangerous choice you should not make, for you could find your life's at stake

The Grind

Awake until the early morning, the new day dark but slowly dawning
With bleary eyes you greet this sight, you want the dark and not this light
To take away this pain and sore, is what you yearn so frightfully for
With no reprieve and no relief, it tests your spirit and belief
It's darkness now you wish to keep, if just for rest and not for sleep
The tiredness of your mind to cease, lying quiet and still in blissful peace
For when you face that daily grind it's this unsettling fact you find
When work becomes your destination you're in a state of desperation
In problems of the day you're mired, a state that leaves you feeling tired
You wish the day would soon be finished and all your stress could be diminished
But when again it's time for bed, well that's the place you sometimes dread
Where all the pain and all the sore comes back to haunt and taunt once more
At times it seems it's such a trial, it's then you'll need to raise a smile
For with a smile you'll ease the way to face the bright and busy day

The Tasks

As days fly by in such a whirl it's in your mind that thoughts will swirl
This constant noise which never ceases now seems to pull you into pieces
Your mind at rest, an endless chatter, no peace with this disturbing clatter
It's of yourself you're forced to ask how you'll complete these endless tasks
For those above who set the goals, think easy are such mundane roles
They set the standards of the norm for work they never will perform
When task performance is disjointed they'll look to see where blame is pointed
With shock they'll state how they're appalled when plans now seem derailed or stalled
There's little care if you seem lost, their care is when they count the cost
They'll change the structure and the name and hope that things won't stay the same
They steer a course for more outsourcing, efficient use with less resourcing
Derailments then can soon turn viral, direction now a downward spiral
They race to reach the lowest bar which seems to you as not that far
It's then you think perhaps you'll say, good luck and now I'll say good day

The Walls

These walls that have me closed within, no halls or warm, inviting inn
Alone with all my thoughts that sway, the way I feel and see this day
A friendly face I long to see, so closeness now may come to me
And I shall not feel so alone, with silence like some mournful drone
And how I wish to feel so much, a truth of strength for me to touch
So tempted now to join the throng with others who feel they belong
Upholding values that they see, no matter what these values be
My will surrendered to the crowd, where I'll proclaim and shout out loud
Yet change they wish to see in me is something I must never be
A servant who shall have no will when troubled thoughts will not be still
A pawn for when they rant and rave as though to them my mind's a slave
To care not how or why they choose the games of power that they will use
Some lesser man that I now see, is what these walls could make of me
Alone you're never truly free, to share is life's contented key

Toxic Leader

When you can feel you're just a number it seems to cause a frown
In bed it's then you'd rather slumber, these feelings bring you down
You'll bring a style to raise a smile and get on with the day
Until too long has been the while that you have had a say
For what you face can seem too hard when care is not displayed
When what's received is disregard, with this you are dismayed
Of care not even some pretence to bend you to their will
How little this can then make sense as motion stalls to still
An arrogance is what you sight in how you're now being treated
To disagree will cause a fight with those who're so conceited
Within your mind this truth you find, this lacking from a leader
When at their core they are unkind distrust becomes their feeder
They feel so right in what they say, with this being their simplicity
But all their overbearing ways bring more of their toxicity

Vice

Is not a vice just but a tool and not a thing to trap a fool
A vice being used to keep in place, to work a task at measured pace
Why is it that this word then changed, how far it seems this word has ranged
Its grip that has such full control now seems to take some other role
What now creates this powerful vice, by where and how, on whose advice
This vice being not what others know, its hold the cause of hidden blows
Yet what we see with powerful vice is pleasure aimed there to entice
It's been this way through every age, promoted as though on a stage
Now impolite, or bluntly crude, dismissive of those deemed as prudes
Sometimes a vice is never found, as though being hidden underground
The place to which all vice you'll send, if vice is what you try to end
With vice you never truly win, it ends and then once more begins
It seems with vice we have to live, until such time we choose to give
For when the world is full of take, a strength to vice is what we make

Wahine – 10 April 1968

From Lyttleton the ship did sail, the course being steered into a gale
In driving rain the vessel showered, to reach safe harbour on she powered
The force of wind to gust and blow, the going now so rough and slow
The journey's end being one of grief, the hull being holed on Barret Reef
The wind swept spray that formed a mist and in this gloom she seemed to list
The flooding caused the power to fail, and now to drift, no more to sail
The harbour's entrance where she grounded, not far from this is where she foundered
Beneath the waves to slowly slip, this sleek-lined inter-island ship
The passengers in a state of shock, on davits did the lifeboats rock
No safer place for them to be than lowered to the raging sea
A fear now felt down to the core, to reach the safety of the shore
The lifeboats hauled up to the beach but safety's shore not all would reach
That fateful day to count the cost of over fifty lives being lost
To hope again there'll never be a storm that brings such deadly seas

Atheist

Oblivion awaits, so the atheist will say, a cold and dark nothing at the end of our days
No more of these feelings of joy or to ache, the emotions of life at the end we forsake
What they see in this life as the only real issue, is how we are beings of flesh and soft tissue
Of blood and of bone but without a true soul, it's these things alone they believe make us whole
And to only the physical do we need to give, as it's only in memories of others we live
For yours are the memories that cannot survive, these are the thoughts that this belief drives
Sometimes it can seem this is stated with pride, as though to be blessed when no longer alive
Their belief in oblivion has a stubborn persistence, it seems that they wish for an end to existence
But some will not listen to talk of such loss, and turn to a temple, a church, or a mosque
Where hope can arise from the deepest of holes, with a spiritual feeling uplifting their souls
No scorn should be shown to those who believe, that all that we love, and will learn or achieve
Is there for a purpose, and when earned at a cost, shall not be forgotten by forever being lost
You need not believe in the one who is all seeing, some singular thing, or esteemed higher being
But all that exists in this place of the physical is balanced and bound by a strength that is spiritual

Blind Faith

The sun as it dawns and the days into nights, such awesome, inspiring, and beautiful sights
A rhythm, a cycle, a season, a miracle, the sights so uplifting and seeming so spiritual
These colours of light, so vibrant and real, being used for expressing the ways that we feel
A red rage of anger, seeming down with the blues, such colourful emotions in the language we use
But when from your birth you have been without sight, how would you imagine these colours of light
The cool shades of blue and the vibrance of red, could you conjure up colours from what has been said
What words of these colours would help to assist, when only in thought can this spectrum exist
Yet the colours are real, with a faith you could say, when you're blind to the light and the sight of the day
With sight so engrained in the lives of all others, being lost in a world of no light and no colours
A faith and conviction must surely then be, in all that there is that you just cannot see
There's a place that is real, to which we're all blind, a space that exists without distance or time
With no physicality of feeling or seeing, a place where we'll know of the spiritual being
A spiritual faith can bring all shades of colours, no longer being blind to the insight of others
It gives us a hope and a feeling of charity, that into our lives can come meaning and clarity

Complexities of Belief

Some come to feel it's been awhile, belief in one true being
Of this they cannot reconcile, with all that they are seeing
An explanation of some sort of what to them God means
Does not resemble what was taught, such visions now unseen
To wish to feel a truth now found, their doubts being left behind
Of definition strong and sound, with this their thoughts are lined
A universal energy, diversity of kind
Of nature being in synergy with all sub-conscious mind
An energy that seems so abundant, through this all life persists
So much to spare but none redundant, in all that now exits
Energy stored in molecules, in minerals turned to stone
In scale or skin or follicles, in flesh and blood and bone
An energy that feels underrated in how it seems employed
Its ways that see all life created, to fill the darkened void.

Creation

From nothing came that great big bang, some say it's how all life began
That all of life had its gestation within this light that was creation
When thinking all is evolution, in thought we need a revolution
For with creation life then evolved, to be the sights we now behold
What came to be has us enthralled and to its wonders we are called
Smaller parts of a greater being, creation now being all we're seeing
From first dawn's glow the world revolving, and life on earth with time evolving
It's to adaptation life was bound, from ancient seas then on the ground
In all of this we're not alone, we have not evolved on our own
In other worlds we then may find there's other life of conscious mind
But to such thoughts some feel adverse and cannot see this universe
As one creation that makes the whole, with life the thing that forms the soul
Evolving life will spread and grow and seeking minds will come to know
That you and I and all we're seeing, are part of some great higher being

DNA

Some say that people have no soul and life is just to play a role
Of randomness they seem so sure, and after life there is no more
They proudly state there's no solution, no purpose for our evolution
No reason for a thinking mind, and at our deaths these truths we'll find
Yet what to find we will not know if all that death to us will show
Is darkness with a cold persistence, no thoughts or feelings with non-existence
If there's no reason for our lives, why is it then that we will strive
And question how we have evolved, then wish this puzzle to be solved
When traced back through our DNA, how we've come here is hard to say
From where we came the journey's long, and through its trials it's made us strong
Our DNA makes us unique, a fact of science with much mystique
Genetic paths although related, as individuals we are created
There is no other just like you, to see the things the way you do
So find your place and know the role that fills the purpose of your soul

Doctrines

So starkly seems a message turned, much less now of forgiving
So many by such doctrines spurned, in ways in which they're living
Compassion and a caring found, it's this that's truly sacred
But now we find such doctrines bound, by judgement causing hatred
God's children we are all as one, through God we are created
But when you judge it's love you shun, with difference strongly stated
What of these words seen written down, the ones of said disciples
With judgement that can bring a frown, these verses, and recitals
To some they feel it's not so real, these words seem like betrayal
For with such words how then to heal, this judgement seems so stale
Have we not seen all those who rave, of righteousness and might
As though to judgement they're some slave, and how they know they're right
How can this be what Jesus taught, of ways to be as lovers
These doctrines that seem filled with faught, with little care for others

Evil Deeds

All the while an unholy lust, a deceitful smile when breaching trust
To evil deeds an active creditor, concealing actions of a predator
As though they cannot deal with shame but who they hurt are scarred and maimed
Their wounds severe and scoured with salt, when those to blame admit no fault
No thought or care of souls to tend, of shattered trust to try to mend
The weak and vulnerable being cast aside for wicked sins some wished to hide
But they alone are not betrayed, inaction affecting all who prayed
That those involved would see the need to stop these acts and evil deeds
No threats to them of endless fire, it's in denial we find they're mired
Facts and truths being buried or fudged, so Mother Church shall not be judged
But those with strength who have survived, for justice they have longed and strived
A virtuous challenge they choose to mount, to hold the sinful to account
No more will this now be allowed, despicable acts being disavowed
A moral wealth which now seems spent, so strongly how should they repent

Faith In Love

Why does it state so in the Bible, for evil we were all held liable
As though there's evil in a child, a thought that leaves some feeling riled
They can't believe in sacred verses that aim at us these dreadful curses
A faith in God they should not tell, through frightful tales of torturous hell
To be cast down as though a thief and punished with some unjust grief
With pleasure's sin being held to blame, as though we're filled with lust and shame
It seems this god we must hold dear is not of love but one of fear
Through fear we will not wish to stay, so from this god we turn away
The one of love being which we seek, a god that shall protect the weak
A caring god of restitution and not one of great retribution
For it's through love that we are strong and with this love we all belong
To problems love will bring solutions, and through this love a revolution
We shall not seek a god to fear, the god of love we will hold dear
This faith in love to soothe the soul, that lifts us up and makes us whole

God Of Love

Those with a love for a faith with cruel traits, have little concern for the fears they create

The passion they find in the pain of the rod, the greatness of power from a harsh vengeful god

With theirs being the god to which all must be turning, or we shall have souls that forever are burning

Cast down to the depths of some low torturous hell, it's these and more tales of such anguish they'll tell

They base an obedience on enhancing your fears, or inflicting a pain that will bring you to tears

Through all of the ages some seemed to be willing, to wallow in blood as they did their god's killing

If this is religion to some it rings hollow, for a god full of love is the one they would follow

When fear is being used for a soul to be swayed, it's from these beliefs that they'll then turn away

No rapture but rupture and deepening displacement, a solace now sought through a spiritual replacement

Disposing of values for riches with gladness, embracing the want of their greed without sadness

Self-serving promotion that forgoes the good deed, the profit of money being the god they now heed

Small peace of mind will be what this wealth brings, while money may talk it's your soul that can sing

Who knows what to make of religious belief, when those who have faith say they find great relief

When all you would wish from the spirit above is the strength and the power of a god full of love

Hallelujahs

Of hallelujahs they would sing in tones of ringing joy
Of all the memories this would bring when you were just a boy
The Sunday message told in books, well-schooled in love, and caring
And how it was the way it looked, that all was there for sharing
An innocence that soothed your soul, no judgement or demanding
No burning fire or deep dark hole, not cursed and not commanding
A gentleness with stories told, of trials being overcome
And how with this your soul seemed sold to whom they named the son
But none of this remained the same, you found as you got older
For tales were then of whom to blame, a warmth now seemed much colder
For blame's the thing you wished to shun, a new page and new day
This coldness it should never come, to you not in this way
You think back on that time long passed, when you were just a child
The shame that sharing could not last, now all the world seems wild

Heaven And Hell

Of heaven's heights or depths of hell, some can't believe these tales they tell
And all those visions that they'll bring, of angels dancing on the wing
Of demons in an endless fire, it's of these tales they never tire
With threats against your sacred soul being made to keep you in control
The power they hold, some now can see, restricts, and does not set you free
As warnings are such tales being told and through a fear is how they're sold
And with this fear they'll then proclaim that you'll be cursed, and damned, and shamed
But feeling fearless makes you think, bring all your curses to the brink
You'll then refuse some frightful frown from those in power to keep you down
Whose thoughts of God seem so mistaken, let all their curses be forsaken
For God is love and that is all, no demons here to make you fall
God is love and love is real, with love the thing that lets you heal
We're each the seeker of our soul, and share this love that makes us whole
And it is God that keeps us strong, this god of love where we belong

Holy Wars

The clergy used the sponge of youth to soak in what they deemed as truth
To agitate and breathe the drama while dressed in ways of unseen armour
A scheming stealth to then persuade to join and fight some cruel crusade
How they instilled into young minds of all the fears that they could find
For with these fears came full control, a stake being planted through the soul
The young being seen as wilful starters, for holy wars prepared as martyrs
That they should pray unto their Lord that they could be God's vengeful sword
And those they seek to fight and slay be mired in depths where they will lay
The drums to beat a powerful rattle, the stage then set for righteous battle
With empty failings to be filled by those deserving to be killed
To speak of God was there a lie to say these others now must die
As what for God shall you then win when you engage in mortal sin
From mortal blows that cause such harms, this thought before you set to arms
From hatred we will rise above when we accept God's gift of love

Holy Water

The sun to bring its heat to flow and melt away the ice
From water then it's life that grows, with fields of wheat and rice
To life this water gives is its gift and seeds are set for sowing
It's life that water will uplift, abundance to be showing
From shallow seas first life to form, this water world the womb
Through eons life to be the norm, life's time on land to loom
The empty land so warm and moist, of barrenness now changing
How life adapts through chance and choice, its seeds forever ranging
Where water will begin to flow, to life it brings its force
This water how it then shall show, of life it is the source
For water makes the desert bloom, of sand being turned to sod
As though to fill an empty room, this water that's of God
The waves of life to reach the crest, through water being baptised
This holy water has us blessed, our spirits then to rise

In God's Name

To speak of God there can be found some small dislike for how this sounds
This word to some is not respected, what once believed is now rejected
For in God's name were many sores, from inquisition to holy wars
And those who say they're on God's mission, can cause great rifts and deep division
They say of God we must have fear, of endless fire where souls will sear
This power and glory full of might, seems less for love and more for fright
And those who wish to save your soul, it's of your life they want control
Their rules by which all must abide when from their god you cannot hide
Where all being held up for to blame, mean less than those who can be shamed
When shamed it's soon that they'll obey, while those being blamed keep well away
The message seems to some distorted, with troubles never solved or sorted
What god could there now ever be, to wish this hate and war we see
When God is love is what is real, true freedom is what you will feel
It's from our love this hate won't steal, when God is love it's then we heal

Rome

Great temples and majestic halls, the Colosseum with blood-stained walls
So many gods at once revered, but if opposed enslaved or speared
For those with lives so subjugated, contempt and scorn for them created
Yet within the walls of ancient Rome there stands the Church's sacred home
The martyrs held the mob enthralled, with love the message they installed
Nor more would crowds accept the cost of games being held where lives were lost
From ancient gods Rome breaks and lurches, to form the mother of all churches
An empire with a changed perspective, of sacred souls to be protective
And this new faith it spoke of rest, a sacred place where souls are blessed
How it is God that you forsake if one day's rest you will not take
When rest won't come until the grave, you live a life where you're enslaved
These tales of faith then seemed to be such stories told to set them free
Within our lives and high above most sacred is the gift of love
An end to life we should not dread, the message of this faith was spread

Spirit Time

To be enthralled by life's great mysteries, what's been before and now are histories
This grip some feel from life's strong force and how they wish to know its source
Like gravity it forms attraction, their thoughts they wish to turn to action
So keen they seem to wish to find a universal subconscious mind
Of spirit time to now elect, to free the mind and then connect
With spirits of the universe is where they wish to feel immersed
Of limits now to be transcending, to see themselves as though ascending
Restrictiveness to be undone when all subconscious minds are one
To know they'll find that what they face is bright with light and filled with grace
As though subconscious thought can be the way to change the world we see
To view once more in awe and wonder, life's rhythms beating loud as thunder
To seek the answers to help explain this universe and our domain
This universal energy, when tapped can truly then flow free
To spirit time they give their thought, subconscious mind, clear vision sought

Spiritual Energy

If the energy that's formed in a meteor shower, should strike at the earth with a destructive power

All over the globe could the damage extend, and much of the life on our world could then end

Energy so powerful that it shatters and shocks, yet the energy in matter can seem to be locked

The energy of atoms in the frame of a door, seeming static and still, yet they make up the core

Such energy's inert and sits low where it lies, while that which can move has an energy that's high

This simplest of truths that has now been instilled, all things have an energy with which they are filled

But a spiritual energy is a thing that you find, which you'll come to know when you open your mind

A spiritual sight can make dreams seem majestic, our thoughts giving energy to what is suggested

This spiritual energy that can make us feel whole, the store of your thoughts being the core of your soul

An energy that's real but in a spiritual form, expanding and deepening from the day you were born

For some it now seems there's a truth they can sight, there are two types of energy that now bring the light

With one made of matter that creates our surrounds, and the spiritual energy that can know of no bounds

What we see, hear, and feel made up of the physical, enhanced by the uplifting strength of the spiritual

While all that is physical can crumble and fall, it's the spiritual energy that forever stands tall

State Of Mind

Religion seems a state of mind, but those with faith sometimes you find
Can have beliefs to which they're sworn that leaves you with your conscience torn
For some there seems no loving god, but one well-known for wrath and rod
To butcher, burn, and scar and maim, all of this done in their god's name
To distrust some will choose to teach and hate can then be what they preach
Threats and fears to be embellished, as though to harm's the thing to relish
With malice they will then divide and claim that God is on their side
To rage against some moral sin, yet set to war and hope to win
But in our mouths the taste is sour if love is lost for the sake of power
When this distaste's too hard to swallow, then in this faith we will not follow
No more of hawks, please bring the dove, and talk of kindness and of love
So darkened days in time will end, and light-filled life will shine again
That conflicts past are put to rest, it's well we need to pass this test
And with these thoughts you then may find that love can change your state of mind

The Balance

To some the days we spend on earth seem time being lived before our birth
Of trials and tests upon our soul to form the strength that makes us whole
And those with hearts to evil sworn will fail this test and not be born
Nor those immersed in rampant greed whose actions make a curse of need
True souls being formed through gifts of love, from deep within and high above
Where those who give shall pay the price when love requires some sacrifice
With this we find the truth of measure does not rely on gold or treasure
For if you've sold your soul to wealth then this will take its toll on health
When time is spent being to employ such deeds that bring with them a joy
It brings a balance to our lives, this joy for which we all should strive
The harvest that you then will reap are memories which you long to keep
To be the host of gentle dreams where sense is made of how things seem
In light-filled life we wish to bathe, through fields of strife to cut a swathe
No paths to conflict to be trod, the balance sought as though through God

The Godless

When dreadfully cruel are the things that we see, a god full of love some will say there can't be

A world full of greed now so scarred and defiled, the cold hand of death that takes hold of a child

Of nature that's powerful yet random in course, creating great havoc through a destructive force

Where most living things will each face the day, by being the predator or becoming their prey

How even the trees as they grow seem to smother, with sunlight being dimmed by a dense foliage cover

A world full of want being the cause of all wars, no miracles now that will heal all these sores

To reach such an age that will leave you with sighs, with far fewer hellos and so many goodbyes

Where now there is loss where once there was gain, life's closest companion being some chronic pain

And all that is loved with such sweetness and joy, the long march of time can seem set to destroy

How dreadful your plight when you're left all alone, to cause you to cry or so softly to moan

Of a god full of love some remain unconvinced, godless when born they have been this way since

For what are the stories that heaven can tell, when life can at times seem like some kind of hell

Surrounded by dark they are blind to the light, their eyes cannot see with a spiritual sight

To take in the beauty and with faith then to say, that all is renewal, and rebirth is God's way

The Good Book

Without your path devoid of vice, a path with loss and sacrifice
The message that they seem to preach, that paradise lost is out of reach
These sinful acts for which you're liable, as stated so there in the Bible
Can leave you feeling unendorsed, and then to be without remorse
As though with hope there is no glimmer, and you remain a mortal sinner
These words of which you once were shown now being the things you cannot own
This book that starts with Genesis, how truly strange it seems this is
Six days to make this world at best with the seventh day being one for rest
It seems a book that's full of fables, like the one of Cain and Abel
When human beings could stoop no lower a tale is told of floods and Noah
Yet while it seems so full of curses, it speaks of love in many verses
And all those proverbs without pretence, talk of plain truths and common sense
Within your mind this plants a seed, of questions you will now take heed
You wonder where your path will lead when of this book you choose to read

The Puzzle

Were we created or did we evolve, it seems like this question can never be solved
Life as creation or just evolution, it appears that we're destined to have no solution
And then there's the faith that each can perceive, to be the persuasion which all should believe
But some will then wish for our mouths to be muzzled, for daring to speak of or question this puzzle
Yet others believe both views to be right, with life being created by a heavenly sight
An explosion of light so brilliant and radiant, the first forms of life with the proton gradient
Clouds full of gases and a world warm and moist, life slowly adapting with freedom and choice
Through natural selection all life then evolves, to overcome problems and for puzzles to solve
The puzzle of that of our physical place, the puzzle when gazing far out into space
The puzzle of people's desire for proximity, contrasting with that of no end to infinity
The physical and spiritual never truly can join, with these like opposite sides of a coin
And this is a coin that is spent at great cost, with its value attained when our lives can seem lost
Some will declare that there's no hope of seeing, an answer to the question of the spiritual being
But I see no puzzle in need of being solved, as there was a creation and then we evolved

Virtue

Some with faith may see so clearly the story of the Virgin Mary
A newness to this tale of old, and truth to them of how it's told
A story of great strength through virtue and how such strength shall never hurt you
With virtue being the righteous way, the path that does not lead astray
We all are virgins at our birth, from a mother's womb to greet the earth
And at our birth being loved so much, our innocence as yet untouched
Pure virtue is the virgin's way, but in this state we cannot stay
And what we see as true and just can seem defiled through greed and lust
With some you'll find their conscious thought is where true righteousness is sought
Self-righteous is what they become, with virtue being the thing they shun
And those who seem so sanctimonious, whose self-belief they gladly show to us
Such pride it does not leave them humble, their stride it soon becomes a stumble
Though virtue is the virgin's way and how the threads of virtue fray
To virtue we should all attest as it's with this we'll find our best

Introspection and Reflection

Age of Wisdom

Some say there's wealth that shines like gold, the knowledge of the wise and old
As though for us what comes with age is wisdom that makes some a sage
A teacher of what's wise and prudent to those who wish to be a student
Of that which comes from understanding when challenge can become demanding
Of how to deal with calm and grace when stress or troubled times are faced
Where calmness then can bring to you the path that's right for you to choose
For it's with age that some can find there seems an inner peace of mind
Considered and at times reflective, of mental health to be protective
An age when you will come to know that life has rhythms that ebb and flow
And while success shall make us strive there's more than this to being alive
Of all the struggles that we fear, that seem to us need all our care
Of these you often come to see, things end up how they're meant to be
With age you're not so quick to move, but then you find there's less to prove
Emotions seeming highly strung, best being left for those still young

Change

The place that was from where you came, sometimes you wish had stayed the same
Its comfort felt so close and warm and for its loss you now could mourn
At times it's hard to deal with change as what is new can seem so strange
But this you find may move your mind and shift the way your thoughts are lined
Uplifting things you then may see, a change of scene where you feel free
Of what seems stale to trim or cut, new paths replace those well-worn ruts
Change that's more than some stale sequel, a changed belief to make us equal
Where all who set to work and strive can make real difference to their lives
A swiftness or a creeping change, few limits to where change may range
When common law became the letter, a change through time that made lives better
Replacement or some new addition at times in conflict with tradition
A balance sought and then created so change shall not be overstated
Some different way to then be eased so those in doubt may be appeased
It need not be some fearful thing, embrace this change for what it brings

Chasing Dreams

That different world than of today which now can seem so far away
What's been before and come what may, it's of that world you'd wish to stay
For there you had a comfort known, with love the thing so freely shown
A place you never felt alone, from seeds of love a strength was grown
That love which made you feel so proud now seems it's covered with a shroud
Of clearness turned to mist and cloud, with silence that can seem so loud
The more you move the more you mope, constricted as though tied with rope
Your reach is more a grasp for hope, the only thing with which to cope
Yet hope's the thing that now is seen, much more than on a crutch to lean
Of all there is and what has been, the path you choose is of your dream
No more of feeling sad and blue, it's now you know what you must do
Your dream to make so right and true, this seems the course that's set for you
Procrastination now a race as actions swarm to gather pace
Of all those fears you'll turn and face, when dreams become real things to chase

Childhood Home

You think back to your childhood home and how it now sits all alone
Of childish dreams and expectations, of happy times and tribulations
How life seemed easy, far from hard, when playing in the sun-filled yard
Excitement there to fill the day, with fun being had in simple ways
Of dealing with those growing pains, of cosiness in wind-swept rain
The years of cheers from festive toasts, of family time with Sunday roasts
To care and share that was the norm, a comfort that made feelings warm
This strength of feeling you have stored, of heartfelt times to want for more
As though to wish times past could stay, and parents would not pass away
It's memories now that you must save of all the love they gladly gave
To feel the love within the heart, so strongly given from the start
Of paths for you which they had laid through sacrifices that they made
You look back at the life you had and though at times your thoughts seem sad
You learned to know the life you live depends upon the love you give

Childishness

Of all the things remembered first, from early childhood days
Was how he flowed beneath the dirt, a worm now being his ways
An old, deserted chicken coop is where he met the ground
He burrowed down then made a loop, a flowing movement found
It's how he moved beneath the soil, this simple way to feel
An ease of movement without toil, how this had seemed so real
And as he grew he still remembered how true this seemed to be
As though of limbs to be dismembered and yet to flow so free
A wonderous thing where childhood seems that all such things can be
How thoughts and feelings flow like streams from all that you can see
To put away such childish thoughts they say we all must do
And yet a playfulness of sorts can bring such joy to you
No serious side that seems so stale, no woes to bring you down
An open breeze on which to sail, a smile and not a frown

Complimentary Insecurities

We each can seem to have a sense, of what is real, without pretence
But things of which some won't confide are issues that they choose to hide
They never see the light of day, these hurts securely locked away
As though they're full of dark impurities, creating fears and insecurities
Their shame can leave them inconsolable; they think it weak for feeling vulnerable
It's how they feel they shall appear if they expose their deepest fear
Through strong emotions they can find that guilt and fear controls their mind
And with this they can seem to stumble, and then their walls may seem to crumble
Yet they should not feel pessimistic as only those who are narcissistic
Will see themselves in shining light, so certain that they're always right
Few are the fears such people share, of others they have little care
When in their way they'll push and shove as they're the only one they love
We all have fears down deep inside, from these we should not wish to hide
No need to guard them like a sentry, to share your fears is complimentary

Confronting The Past

To burrow down as though a mole and feel those thoughts of pain
To find so deep within your soul, the past has caused a stain
Discoloured are the brightest lights, as though being cloaked in grey
Some joyfulness you wish to sight, no more of bleak dismay
Confronting though the past may be, it's this that you must face
And then at last the light you'll see, while feeling joy's embrace
So have no fear of what has been, of this there is no shame
We all have troubles that we've seen, true healing's without blame
There's others that you seem to find pretend they have no fear
But well you know that on their mind are things they will not share
So easy it can seem to be, believing in a brilliance
But what that takes you now can see, is strength through your resilience
So now declare down to your core, it's this you must confess
Resilience, you have more in store, so much you now possess

Conspiracy Theory

Conspiracy some will say exists, that through it all falsehood persists
To disbelieve it's now you must for there can be no faith in trust
They say it's all about control, to take our minds and steal our souls
Yet freedom is what they despise when they will broadcast all their lies
They sternly state what's now the cause and have no care for rules and laws
It's others who must toe the line while they'll refuse to pay some fine
When truth's the thing they always query they then agree upon a theory
Where truths are for the mindless herd who cannot see these as absurd
And when united in distrust then all they see can seem unjust
Of others they will show no care, the choice they make being not to share
Yet how is this a way to live, to be conceited and not to give
What is this culture some will crave where fear will make them feel they're brave
No matter now how hard they try their fear creates the biggest lie
Their rants and raves become so dreary, conspire for us another theory

Doubt

In times of stress and strife we find in life we struggle to be kind
As all the things we see and hear can seem to cause us doubt and fear
Important to your mental health is showing kindness to yourself
For when your mind is full of doubt frustration's speech becomes a shout
The cause of doubt within yourself, you park or put this on the shelf
But when your fears you wish to face it's then you'll find that calming place
And with this calm you'll come to know the kindness others then will show
Such lowly doubts that there have been are then replaced with high esteem
For in esteem we all are held, when fears are faced, and doubts are shelved
When fear will plant its doubting seed of this we have small use or need
It's of these things we come to know when we allow our strengths to grow
And how that when we're feeling strong we walk the paths where we belong
So with yourself be calm and kind, it's then that you will come to find
That of those doubts there in your mind, it's these that you now leave behind

Empty Roads

It's when you drive down empty roads, those ones that twist and wind
That you will find such lightened loads bring calmness to your mind
To wish to be no other place, so empty yet not bare
But full of freedom's open space with beauty there to share
The chatter of your thoughts to cease, it's this that you will find
And how you'll feel an inner peace, a stillness to your mind
A solitude that binds your soul as you enjoy the drive
This emptiness that makes you whole, no care where you'll arrive
So gentle is the panorama that takes your stress away
No more some cause to bring a drama, such stillness to the day
And when the sun will bring a gleam to all the natural features
This soothing calmness seems serene, just one of nature's creatures
No one to steal these long, sweet days, no tiresome tasks to tend
Your thoughts now turn to rest and play, of time you wish to spend

Facing Fears

We wish to feel within our lives the sense that we belong
 So deeply does this feeling lie, from there it makes you strong
But with this strength can come fragility, through depth of such emotions
Your mind it seems creates ability to form some foolish notions
As only just the slightest sense can bring to you perception
That what you see is just pretence and you have faced rejection
But of these feelings now being faced that bring you close to tears
Emotions are so easily traced to never facing fears
For when you have such insecurity of which you wish to bury
Then melancholy seems a surety, no mind for feeling merry
To cope can seem to be the thing, to thoughts of this you're giving
It's this which insecurities bring, some fractured way of living
No more should all your fears be shunted, to then be locked away
It's now these fears shall be confronted to bring the bright new day

Freedoms

The freedoms where you get to choose the ways and means of how you'll lose
Are freedoms where you then will find your future has been undermined
The freedoms where they'll shout and hail their slogans with the message stale
Are freedoms that can make you sigh, or bring a pain that makes you cry
When what we see seems some mistake it's of this world no sense we'll make
But freedoms where you'll keep the love when in your face it's hate they shove
Are freedoms that we know can bring the power to make our voices sing
The freedoms where you'll feel no fear but hold each other close and dear
Are freedoms of the human race, bestowed to us through love's sweet grace
These freedoms they can form the key, to change this strife-torn world we see
So freedom is not cruelly styled as though some mean demonic child
Corrupted power no longer craved, no more the poor to seem enslaved
It's on our future fortune smiles when freedom is not of the wild
With thoughts of care we then can choose that freedom's there for all to use

Fungi

It's fungi that you now have tried on trays like some hors d'oeuvres
You're not sure if your eyes have lied as more are being served
The magic mountain you then climb, this dormant, coned volcano
Strange visions whirl within your mind, as though some thought tornado
These vibrant colours bring you awe, full of majestic light
Such wonderous things now to the fore, that makes for altered sight
Of clear, concise, and captured vision being etched upon your mind
As though from depths you now have risen, with freedom there to find
And how this fungi makes you move to rhythms of the soul
With music you seem in the groove and all the room seems whole
You now know why they say it's fungi, that all of us should try
At first you float and then you fly, your mind seems on a high
To see the dark now turned to dawn to bring the bright new day
To feel yourself as though reborn in such a special way

Happy Days

When into states of stress you lurch for peace of mind you'll keenly search
Emotions can seem scarred and raw with thoughts and feelings pained and sore
Those happy days are what you seek, such blissful states again to greet
A place devoid of cold resentment where what you feel is sweet contentment
And to this place some come alone, this peace they'll find when on their own
Seclusion others can't condone and share their all with feelings shown
When stress and strain can be relieved then peaceful calm may be achieved
Which brings the wish to be invited to leave this calm and feel excited
And what excites you'll then explore, this sense that makes you wish for more
It's feelings now not thoughts you heed, for feeling joy is what you need
These happy days that we all chase, to feel again their warm embrace
These times can seem so brief and fleeting, but in your life they bring such meaning
To feel the sense that soothes your soul which fills you up and makes you whole
That calms and stills the frazzled nerve, these happy days we all deserve

Helping Hands

How strange it seems to share your fears with strangers who've been trained to care
To seek the answers they'll provide to all those fears you lock inside
To share those thoughts that take their toll, the ones there deep down in your soul
Where at your core they will attack, with fears that steer you off the track
But there are no answers they can give, no clear direction on how to live
Yet still you'll listen to what they say and hope to find some easier way
The answers that have truth you'll find are those that sit within your mind
It's to the fore they'll then be drawn when calm acceptance begins to dawn
Forgiveness sows the seed of reason, this change of mind being like a season
From winter's gloom to summer's glow, it's then the light will start to show
Your feelings now being understood, to leave your fears can feel so good
Some joyful times are what you seek, these joys that make our lives complete
When guided through with helping hands your path seems clear for making plans
You'll sight the light and then you'll know, to love yourself and let things go

Homestead

What were the loves and hopes and dreams that filled your grey and tired
    old beams
You stand alone flayed by the breeze, your rustic charm seems bent with ease
Your chimney that made cold rooms warm now lies upon what once was lawn
Your timbers brittle, frail, and worn, a home to where the termites swarm
Your windows looked on history's page as progress leapt or change was staged
To share the view from a windowsill of change that never could be still
The tides of time your purpose stole as changes took their lonely toll
Within your walls there's now no soul, abandoned has become your role
Of thoughts of care you've been deprived, to this sad state you have survived
In wind your timbers creak and groan, your walls no longer make a home
Yet what we see as long decay was strong with love that made the day
At times being filled with joy and laughter and warmed by dreams of ever after
A place of timber, brick, or stone, no matter if you stay or roam
Where love is strong and freely shown it's this that truly makes a home

Kapiti Coast

Those drives which you enjoyed the most, your journey's end the Kapiti Coast
With sausage wrapped in warm bread rolls it's to the beach we then would stroll
Those sun-filled days with little cloud, contented best described the crowd
Of loftiness held high or hallowed, no care to spare, all thoughts were shallow
The sand was never seen as golden, but beauty had your eyes beholden
Kapiti Island, untouched, serene, with bush-clad hills and waters clean
The native species of the tree, for bird life now a sanctuary
So close the island seemed to be as though you'd wade across the sea
When settling down upon the beach most other thoughts seemed out of reach
While clearly there to rest and laze, those crowded thoughts being lost in haze
To soak in sun's sweet warming rays and feel there'd be no better days
The salty scent within the air, the time being spent without a care
And when no matter what we'd try, a breeze would make umbrellas fly
It never seemed to make you sigh, you'd smile and set back down to lie

Leaving

Changed heart, changed pace, new start to face, new goals to chase
To ease your mind, you leave behind, more love to find
No reason now to stay here, no longer do you hold dear, no need to ever feel fear
When all you want is to share and to dare
So move now, for now you need to show how
That you have got the low down and how you will not slow down, from fears frown
To know what's real, how fear can steal the way you feel
Leave all your fright, strong light you'll sight, now feel its might
So take it, you know you're going to make it, to stay seems just to fake it
This cage you need to shake it, then break it
To feel free, with all the things that will be, no cages now will you see
To be, me is your key
With all it stole, it took its toll, new life, new role
These paths so long, but now you're strong, where you belong

Loneliness

With loneliness you think you find for you there is no care
It plays these tricks upon your mind and seems so hard to bear
It cuts its way down to your soul and fills up your surrounds
To make you feel you're less than whole, a void by which you're bound
It's then you'll wish some place to run, to take you from the dark
Sometimes when you will greet the sun, your loneliness seems stark
A faith in love is what you need, that drives away despair
Of dark-filled voids to take no heed, as kindness will appear
Through love you won't feel all alone, as others they will share
It's love that you will then be shown when of your soul you bare
No more these thoughts of how for you that no one else will care
You know such thoughts were never true as they now disappear
You feel at once your spirits lift, to ease your state of mind
This life is such a short, sweet gift, and joy is there to find

No Fear

There is a truth where you will find those thoughts that lie within your mind
Will change the way how things can be and different outcomes then you'll see
The thoughts where fear is now refused, with courage being the thing that's used
No thoughts by which you are controlled nor anxious doubt that leaves you cold
When all that makes you wise and good is to the fore and understood
Your will can seem as hard as rock as of your strengths you now take stock
It's fear that makes you feel a fool, but fear can also be a tool
Against these fears you are protected when strength is what is now projected
When you allow your self-belief it's then you'll find that sweet relief
As all your strengths will then unfold and change the way your story's told
When what you face is with a calm it's fear that you will then disarm
A stillness where you'll make your stand, and then to deal with what's at hand
The plainest truths ring strong and true, the outcomes then are up to you
No fear will ever make you fold so now's the time for feeling bold

Normal

When trouble sits within your mind some say that you're not normal
Too much of this and then you'll find such statements made are formal
It's then you'll see just how you're labelled when you can't cope with stress
That you are deemed as not well abled, within yourself you're less
To join a group your fate seems cast, a group not like the others
When of their tests you did not pass it seems inclusion smothers
Yet what's so normal in what we see when strife will fill the world
It seems such trouble's come to be, fear's banner being unfurled
A normalness for states to plunder, of times to fight and war
A normalness to times of hunger, with pain being to the fore
A normalness for ruthless leaders obsessed with all their vanity
Corruption's course becomes the feeder for cruelties and calamity
So as for normal some confess this state is not their favourite
Quite happy to be seen as less, at times they seem to savour it

Of Mystery And Magic

In long-lost times and ancient days the oceans were a secret
And while we longed to know their ways these sparkling seas would keep it
What lay beneath the ocean's waves to all was just a mystery
This knowledge for which some would crave with longing throughout history
Strange stories seeded in our minds inspired imagination
Great monstrous beasts we then could find caused more than agitation
The essence of the ancient world, of mystery and of magic
Displease the gods and risk being hurled to deaths far more than tragic
And then to view a sea of stars, like lanterns on a stage
But not to know how near or far, these stars that make an age
To wonder etched deep in our souls, this magic we were seeing
To plot our course and know our role, so strong within our being
No longer now can magic be with facts and figures rendered
To some it seems a shame to see that ancient times have ended

Other Worlds

Not long ago you were seen as deranged if ever you tried to convince or explain

Of what you believe and would strongly insist, that on other worlds life must surely exist

As this was a time to dismiss the unknown, we're the only ones here and we stand all alone

For we were created, with our lives being unique, and other opinions you never should seek

That insular thoughts must somehow be turned; this seems a lesson that some have now learned

A freedom of thought like a curtain being lifted, consistent closed views being opened and shifted

The question to pose that some can now see, would alien life seem familiar to me

Of this some would say they are perfectly sure, whatever we lack they are bound to have more

As much of the time on our world has been spent with life coming back from extinction events

To look for comparison it's then we may find in terms of development we are now far behind

Perhaps there's a truth that someday we may face, that an alien life is a much-advanced race

If this were the case, could we then come to see, our strength being close to the wild is the key

Of our special world we must treat it with care, and then venture out without worry or fear

To see what there is of this life and then more, when these other worlds we will come to explore

Peace of Mind

To feel the sun's warm shining rays as one we all enjoy these days
Its light a beacon to behold, its warmth that keeps us from the cold
And with its sight you then can find it brings a balanced peace of mind
When nature's rhythms softly beat within your soul it's calm you'll greet
From anxious thoughts there comes relief and in yourself you'll have belief
Of rising fears they now decline when stillness is the thing you find
Such days that seem so calm and mild can give you hope as though a child
It's your self-worth you'll then assess and not those things that you possess
Possessions have no power to heal in fact at times they seem to steal
To rob you of your time to share and take from you those thoughts of care
Your days on earth the wealth you spend, a wealth that none can give or lend
Of all these things that hold so true, to know of what this means for you
It's peace of mind we all wish for, this want that feels no guilt for more
To search your way through life's grand maze and find you have the best of days

Perceptions

In dark filled fields sometimes I would lie, as though stuck to a paper that catches a fly
I'd feel to the earth that my body was bound, but gone was the feeling of being down on the ground
Up onto its side I felt the earth grabbing me, held there in place and fixed firm from its gravity
As though like a picture pinned up on a wall but feeling no height from which I could fall
Lying still in the dark as my mind seemed to race, when all of the stars I could see there in space
Seemed in reach of my hands and not high in the sky, when up on the side of the earth I would lie
With such an odd sight and unusual perspective my vision would then seem so clear and receptive
Just some tiny speck being held there in place, and not looking up but staring out into space
Not only with sight was there difference to find, strange, altered states would flow into my mind
With all of this vastness my eyes could then see, changing perception with thoughts to run free
That all through the sky so much seemed alive, the stars were like bees and space seemed the hive
Stars making days that are bright warm and sunny, bringing the life which can flow like its honey
This vision is clear and can seem so concise, its the wonders of life that do not have a price
No fees due to pay and no debts to collect, it's nature that's precious and in need of respect

Resistance

Why is it that I have resistance, to wish to raise a smile
Of sadness it seems there's insistence, of gloom it's been awhile
Too quick I've been to rush to trouble, to fill my life with stress
My mind it then becomes a muddle, of this I must have less
So now I wish for sunny days, of outlooks shining bright
A place of warmth where I can stay, fresh feelings seeming light
Those days of rain won't cause me pain, it's how the garden grows
No harsh cruel words shall leave a stain, nor dim the light that glows
When some will wish to push and shove, I'll step out of their way
For now I want to feel the love that brightens up my day
Though things may change they stay the same in what is best to feel
No peace of mind is found in blame, for blame can never heal
Of melancholy I'll resist, no more my thoughts to sway
To pleasant thoughts I'll now enlist and then I'll find my way

Rhythmic Thoughts And Recollections

Rhythmic thoughts and recollections within your mind as though reflections
Retrieving them can leave you humbled when rhyming thoughts can be so jumbled
Bold statements made though not poetic; the picture painted is not aesthetic
When laced with fear or rage and curses, so far from sonnets these rhythmic verses
Of feelings that you have connection, expressing all your introspection
And yet to never feel the time that's spent on thoughts and how they rhyme
Where is it rhythmic thought belongs, in poems or in structured songs
Yet while you'd wish for dash and dapper it's plain to see you are no rapper
Of rhyming words for recollection you write these down and make selection
The first being used are ones that make do and then to see where words will take you
The more you write the more it's seeming, that words being used have changed the meaning
Your mind now far from where you started, as those first thoughts have now departed
Your challenge being a statement made from lists of words on pages laid
With meaning changed and much correction, these rhythmic thoughts, and recollections

Sacrifice

To some it seems that sacrifice is less a virtue and more a vice
Some dreadful things none should be seeing that take the lives of other beings
An evil for which blood will spill until such time it's had its fill
It knows no limits in times of war of this sad fact we can be sure
Down to your bones its cold will chill to take your heart and make it still
It thirsts for victims yet still needs more when all around is draped with gore
With fear being kept down to a frown it's then your life that you lay down
To help protect the lives of others as though being sisters or your brothers
This powerful force of selfless love brought by the hawk and not the dove
Such acts of love you know will hurt you must surely then be more than virtue
Those shells at flesh will maul and ransack but you stand tall for you are Anzac
And the bugle plays that mournful post for those with courage who gave
    their most
For when your boots with steel are shod and with your back straight as a rod
You'll march through fields of mud and sod to climb that crest and be with God

Self-Belief

With some they seek a power through wealth, of fears to find relief
The simplest thing for mental health, the power of self-belief
As while we have the need for money and all that it will buy
It can't bring love as sweet as honey, no matter what you try
It's with a love that we are strong for others and ourselves
And through this love that we belong when fear's the thing we shelve
When wealth can seem a state of mind, of blessings you'll take heed
And with this you can come to find you now have all you need
A strength derived through thoughtful giving and not from what you'll take
You change the way you think of living and fears you now forsake
So think again before you doubt the essence of yourself
Frustration speaks as though to shout and impacts on your health
Through self-belief you'll come to know just what for you is real
A fire within will start to glow and strength is what you'll feel

Self-Worth

Of your self-worth you seem unsure, with others you feel insecure
As though it's they who hold the key to open doors for you to see
A place of freedom where you'll find there's few constraints upon your mind
A strength of will with comfort found, that's not enclosed, by borders bound
Where freedom's strength is what you'll use to know the options you should choose
To know yourself down to your soul, then take the paths that make you whole
But freedom is not what you'll find if in your thoughts you are resigned
That life for you is filled with less, and to yourself your second best
True wealth you'll find is at your core, and not material need for more
When you will feel this wealth within on freedom's journey you'll then begin
No other now can hold the key nor bar the paths that set you free
Obstructed routes no longer blocked, your future's door is now unlocked
The ways you need you now have found, foundations solid, strong, and sound
You change the way in which you live when strength to your self-worth you give

Sleepless Nights

It's late at night the demon calls, with tainted strength it creeps and crawls
And it's your mind it wants to win, to batter down until it's in
A vision now so real and clear which brings to you cold crushing fear
Its frightful face, and dark-filled frown, that ties you up then takes you down
It seems to be some dreadful test, this thing that gives your mind no rest
For restful calm your soul will mourn when sleepless nights then turn to dawn
It's then you'll greet the sun's warm rays, no darkness now with light-filled days
Which to your thoughts can bring distraction when tasks are there for you
 to action
And with these tasks comes peace of mind, if only for some short, sweet time
But all distraction gives is pause and you don't turn to face the cause
This thing with which you now must deal, the cause of all the angst you feel
Which takes your calm, and sleep will steal, to face this is the way to heal
So do not fear that fitful sleep, or maddened mind where you could weep
No matter now the dark night's length, to face your fears will give you strength

Spaced Out

To struggle with what is reality and all its forms of deep disparity
Of power that always seems displayed, of conscience fraught and feelings flayed
Of where to look to find a home so you shall never be alone
And feel the strength that you will need to find out where your path will lead
But to a path you're seeming blind, as always something's on your mind
You find instead your thoughts will race and there can be no change of pace
Of wandering mind there is no cause to halt or now to give you pause
With hope your eyes seem firmly set, for nothing you have gained as yet
And words you hear can leave you cold as you take note of what you're told
There's little now that seems as fair, confused is what's become of care
You cannot bring yourself to think how close it is you're to the brink
As though within there's no control, no freedoms, or a defined role
The blame you feel is on yourself from choices left upon the shelf
You turn away to be alone, direction now the thing unknown

Spending Time

That closing time of last drinks ordered when all affairs are finally sorted
Where all your struggles to achieve have been replaced by the one to breathe
Where breath will leave your body still and death then comes against your will
An end of time you hope you'll face with little fear but more so grace
To think this way some say is morbid, your view of life then being distorted
But if this end you wish to fight a different life you then may sight
To know that time will have no side where you can run or from this hide
A precious thing you should adore, how best to use you must explore
To make a choice is what you face, perhaps to choose some slower pace
To know what you would wish to see from time's constraints had been set free
For when life seems some frantic race being out of time is what you chase
No more to spare when you have died, the rule by which we all abide
A thing that none can ever lend, when time has moved to reach the end
The path of time no will can bend so be wise with the time you spend

Spurned

Behaviour disrespecting rules is only shown by utter fools
And then it seems so hard to mend those things that bind you to a friend
No tools for you to use to fix, no charm at all now in the mix
Not just a slip but more a crash, the sad result of being brash
The harshness of the words when spoken makes trust the thing that seems
    so broken
With all the graces that you lack, your wish that you could take it back
These feelings of such sad regret, of these you simply can't forget
Your words ignored as now they're blocked, and so much more it seems has
    stopped
But it's with hope your mind is driven that sometime soon you'll be forgiven
You wish again you'll speak some more and not confront that cold closed door
Too hard to bear these thoughts of loss, it's with despair you count the cost
No more to feel a warmth and glow, it's with this loss you feel so low
You hope your feelings won't be spurned and trust once more can then be earned
So all again can be the same with lessons learned that caused this pain

Sun-filled Days

When looking at the sun-filled sky I watch the birds so freely fly
And with a short, contented sigh, it's on the grass I choose to lie
With sunlight streaming on my face I wish there'd be no other place
Where I must come and go with haste, this calmness now the thing I chase
Within this park my stress sets sail, the pace I seek is of a snail
There's nothing here where I may fail, my anxious thoughts now seeming stale
No more to rush where I must strive, no more some process I must drive
Much more to life than to survive, it's now the gift to feel alive
To do the deals and pay the bill, like pushing barrows up some hill
Of all these things I've had my fill, this blissful calm now keeps me still
A change of heart this calm then makes, why should I strive for what seems fake
Time to reflect the toll this takes, then shrug this off with just one shake
As nothing now shall spoil this day, for peace of mind is why I stay
To feel relaxed in how I lay while soaking up the sun's sweet rays

Sweet Dreams

With time we have the measured hour that has its own eternal power
This power that seems forever deep when you're immersed in trance-like sleep
When waking thoughts can make it seem that all you see is just a dream
Then what you'll wish for as reality are dreams with visions full of clarity
For in these dreams your mind will dare to see a place where all can share
To know this place that has no bounds, where peace of mind can then be found
And then to feel from high above, the need and gift of selfless love
That through this love it's there you'll find those thoughts and deeds so warm and kind
You linger long in blissful sleep for sleep's sweet dreams you wish to keep
Where all those futures there in store bring joy and with them want for more
From peaceful places you awaken and with these dreams your thoughts are shaken
To find that where your mind has ranged has left you with perceptions changed
And changes then are what you'll make, the way you live being what's at stake
Your future now no one can steal when you decide to make dreams real

Temper

At times when you display your temper it leaves you feeling hollow
When shouting's all that you remember it brings a certain sorrow
This temper that you show and feel, you would not wish to follow
The hurt you caused you hope will heal with care being shown tomorrow
But it's today you need to act, you mustn't leave it longer
Of this it is a well-known fact, the sore will soon get stronger
And then you'll find it seems so hard to get back what you had
With cutting words are feelings scarred, which leaves you feeling sad
It's not of love, but more of pride, that now has caused this pain
Those words that cut, to curse and chide, seem set to leave a stain
Our anger often seems directed to those we love the most
Uncaring is what's now projected, when anger we will host
Of temper you must take control, your feelings understood
Bad temper takes a costly toll and never brings the good

The Amazing Kreskin

Your minds being set in single groove when told by thought you'll see things move
That watch's face, you understand, the task to move the seconds hand
A wind-up watch being sprung with tension, but now no wound-up force to mention
It sits there with its hands being still, to move these hands now seems your will
To free your minds without a fear, suggestions from the puppeteer
Who builds the tension in the room, the time hands move now slowly looms
Being too naive to see what's ordered is on some show that's pre-recorded
Through force of minds the ticking started, and narrow-minded paths were parted
It took some time to understand the movement of that seconds hand
Indeed it was a wonderous lesson, the gift of thought from this man Kreskin
Though long it took to run its course the thing you learned was mental force
For you to know that what you feel has energy that is strong and real
That mental energy has a spiritual form, it's this that now can seem the norm
This balance that you try to find when open is a seeking mind

The Devil In The Shoelace Pie

At first you thought it mushroom pie, but now it seems your eyes have lied
In shoelace pie your tastebuds revel, how can this pie be of the devil
The sweet delights of shoelace pie, of this you say now all must try
For far more joy shall shoelace bring than plainer pies made just with string
This is the pie that you should choose, and not one made with slip-on shoes
It's time to try this special treat, delights not solely for the feet
Of all the pies that you have tried, to shoelace are the tastebuds tied
No more to chide or to admonish, they've finally brought your side of polish
This precious pie of which you'll talk, you'll ramble like your mouth could walk
For such pure pleasure you could die, when you first taste the shoelace pie
Not prince of pies but now the king, shoelace makes the senses sing
But never in some high falsetto, that's for pies made with stilettos
When hunger calls there's now no hurry for pies with mushrooms stewed
    like curry
Those mushroom pies they now seem less, it's shoelace pie that's heaven-blessed

The Verge

When feeling low we then can find those thoughts which lie there in our minds
That with such force will have their say like demons who will have their prey
That you deserve no sense of worth, these demons give that notion birth
They sap your strength and sense of self, you feel you're floundering without help
You're anxious now of seeming weak while nervous tension reaches peak
Yourself the one that you now doubt with fear which brings the urge to shout
When all these maddening thoughts then merge you feel you're on some dreadful verge
With no reserves on which to call you wait there for the crashing fall
And not to know where you will land, on solid rock or shifting sand
Your mind in turmoil and full of fright, you feel there is no end in sight
Some courage is the thing to find to face this unease of your mind
And if this courage is what you seek then of these fears you need to speak
For words can calmly lift the curtain, they shed the weight and ease the burden
The gentler path is the one you'll walk when of your fears you choose to talk

To Wander

Within your life some sense of order can then create a comfort border
Where a numbed unfeeling daily grind is calmly met with an ease of mind
To be content with what's achieved, this being the way to feel relieved
But if success is dulled and hollow, some pointless path seems what you follow
A dead-end road on which to shamble until such time you choose to ramble
In which direction you do not know but feelings saying it's time to go
Perhaps there'll be no change at all, for fear can see intentions stall
What's close and near you do not fear, familiar things, their purpose clear
To leave them now could cause you pain and unknown is what you may gain
A strength of mind you'll need muster or wanting change may lose its lustre
Less daring when you're feeling old, so now's the time for being bold
Of thoughts and feelings to take heed, not knowing now where they may lead
To live your life a different way with freshness to the brand-new day
No time to waste, nor thoughts to ponder, it's now you know it's time to wander

Trauma

To some it seems to burn like fire, to wash away the stain
But of this they will quickly tire, for still the stain remains
It leaves the deepest mark of pain, to bruise down to the soul
It's in this hurt that they have lain, this pain that takes control
A trauma found there at their core, a tear that wounds their love
Of this they want to feel no more, from this to climb above
No more of gloomy depths to delve, where everything seems stark
What they now wish within themselves, to rise above the dark
To strive to find what they could be, of this they feel they should
Some other way they wish to see, it's this that's understood
To truly open up your soul, the only way to cleanse
And how it now makes you feel whole to bare your soul to friends
From friends you'll find a strength through love, at times so true and bright
It's then you'll find you'll rise above, it's then the weight feels light

Trust

Where is the trust that you can see, what trust may there now ever be
When words which seem so easily spoken, make promise now the thing that's broken
This trust we all rely upon leaves emptiness when trust is gone
With promise just some picture painted, and trust the brush that seems so tainted
A fleeting trust, it can't run deep, the trust that's rushed it will not keep
But promise kept can make you whole, when trust will reach down to your soul
We all should have belief in trust, not just a wish but more a must
With trust it's doubt that finds its end when you rely upon a friend
When fear and doubt you'll put behind, the strength of trust you then will find
The gift from trust that shall be shown, that in this world you're not alone
This trust promotes your mental health, to trust in others and yourself
No need to run or now to hide when you have friends close by your side
To ease your mind and let things be, a change for good you then may see
No darkened path or heavy load when trust becomes your chosen road

Wellington

To walk the tracks of rugged hills and feel the air when calm and still
Enjoyment of the ocean's breeze, these sights and senses made me pleased
A screen of dreams that was the Roxy, where make-believe became your proxy
The dramas and adventures shown beneath Majestic Theatre's dome
Where stable times can't last forever when once again the earth would tremor
In past times rock raised from the sea, unlocking land with fault line's key
The harbour still and like a pond, these memories for which I am fond
Its waters clean to swim and sail, until the wind became a gale
For then when nature turned the page the sea would froth and foam with rage
To shelter you would quickly run, but soon again you'd greet the sun
Wellington wild and yet serene with calm and storms so often seen
It's of this place being born and raised, to those who listen I'll sing its praise
And though I left so bold and brash, at times I feel this move was rash
For it's the wildness that I miss, along with days of sun-filled bliss

Words Of Rhyme

Of words that rhyme some quickly tire, their scorn can bring them laughter
While others find that rhyme inspires, words linger long thereafter
Rhyme takes them to that special place where meaning can be flowing
Of raw emotion now to face, from what these words are showing
With words that rhyme, some short and fine, a simpler way of seeing
Within their mind some then can find a happiness of being
When stimulating words excite their message seems uplifting
To leave the dark and bring the light, with melancholy shifting
Of rhyme that speaks of sun-filled days, of calm that seems so still
Of warmth in which to rest and laze, and there to have your fill
Those of words of rhyme that then entwine, as though there's now duality
Where you may wish for spirit time that gives to you some clarity
There's so much that this rhyme can bring, some solace to your soul
For only rhyme can make us sing, as one to then feel whole

www.ingramcontent.com/pod-product-compliance
Lightning Source LLC
Chambersburg PA
CBHW051424290426
44109CB00016B/1425